THE
CHILD
AS A
WORK
OF ART

Books by Bennett Olshaker

The Child as a Work of Art
What Shall We Tell the Kids?

THE
CHILD
AS A
WORK
OF ART

Bennett Olshaker, M.D.

READER'S DIGEST PRESS
Distributed by E. P. Dutton & Co., Inc.
New York   1975

The author wishes to thank the following individuals and publishers who granted permission to quote from their works: Dr. Humberto Nagera of the University of Michigan Medical Center; Dr. Harry F. Harlow of the University of Wisconsin; Dr. Anneliese F. Korner and the *American Journal of Orthopsychiatry*, "Individual Differences at Birth: Implications for Early Experience and Later Development," copyright © 1971 the American Orthopsychiatric Association, Inc., reproduced by permission; Dr. Marshall Klaus and associates, the American Academy of Pediatrics, in *Pediatrics* and *The New England Journal of Medicine;* John Wiley and Sons, Inc., for material from *The Child in His Family,* edited by E. J. Anthony and C. Koupernik, copyright © 1970 John Wiley and Sons, Inc.; and Yale University Press, "Young Children in Brief Separation" by James and Joyce Robertson from *The Psychoanalytic Study of the Child,* Vol. 26 by R. S. Eissler, A. Freud, M. Kris, S. L. Lustman, editors, copyright © 1972.

Published simultaneously in Canada by
Clarke, Irwin & Company Limited, Toronto and Vancouver

Library of Congress Cataloging in Publication Data

Olshaker, Bennett, 1921–
    The child as a work of art.

    Includes bibliographical references.
      1. Children—Management.   2. Child study.
  3. Parent and child.   I. Title.
HQ772.O547   1975   649'.1   74-28094
ISBN 0-88349-047-1

To Thelma

". . . the best is yet to be."

Contents

Acknowledgments

Over a period of years, many sources have contributed to the development of my feelings and thoughts which are expressed in this book. I am indebted to the many children and parents with whom I have worked and from whom I have learned; and to my colleagues, in a variety of disciplines, at the Crippled Children's Unit of the District of Columbia General Hospital.

I am grateful to my mother and father for their devoted care and the opportunities they afforded me. My special thanks go to Dr. Reginald S. Lourie, my "professional" father, whose example influenced my choice of a career.

And last, but certainly not the least, I owe so much to my wife and our sons who have all shared in my efforts, creative and otherwise. I have lived with the four of them and have learned much.

Foreword

I hope that the reader of this volume will recognize that this is not a "how to do it" book, but rather a "think about it" book. My strong conviction is that parenthood is an art. And like other creative efforts, it is not an endeavor in which a "paint by the numbers approach" works very well.

Each newborn infant presents us with an opportunity to function as the parents of a unique human being. We cannot decide how we want him to turn out when he becomes an adult and then follow a specific list of instructions to make him fit our image. We can, however, be aware of some of the general factors involved in child rearing. It is the aim of this book to impart to parents, and especially prospective parents, some of the important needs of children and the most important factors in the relationship between children and their parents.

In rearing a child, we are confronted with a complex task which involves the interaction of the infant's natural endowments with his environment. Being a parent is not an easy job. There are no "perfect" ways to rear children—and there are always a number of uncontrollable conditions and events which

11

make the job of rearing youngsters more difficult. But I believe there is no more important occupation than that of being a caring and devoted parent.

Unfortunately, we can see all about us examples of children who have suffered from varying degrees of parental neglect. The neglected child can be found in the ghetto or in a mansion. The reasons for this negligence may vary, but the fact remains that children suffer when they do not have the time and attention of interested and involved parents.

Prevention is always to be preferred to cure. In the case of emotional maldevelopment, it is often difficult, if not impossible, to undo the harm resulting from deprivation during infancy and childhood. To forestall such undesirable personality development in our offspring, it is important that they be wanted and cared for, and that they *be* with their parents in sufficient quantities of time.

I would beseech each couple to consider thoroughly whether or not they really want to have children. If they do, it should be understood that the proper care of youngsters will require an expenditure of time, energy, interest, and money. It will also entail varying degrees of sacrifice.

No infant asks to be born. Once conceived and delivered into this world, he has every right to expect he will be lovingly cared for and guided from his totally dependent state of infancy to adulthood. No one can know ahead of time what a particular baby's temperament will be, whether he will be physically well coordinated, or what assets or liabilities he will possess. But no matter what his make-up, each infant needs the care and attention of adults on whom he can learn to trust and depend. The period of infancy is especially significant in establishing the underpinnings for a person's future life and development. The young child who has his dependency needs filled will become the adult who develops a true feeling of independence.

The infant needs a close attachment to another human being. For optimal growth and development, he requires a sufficient amount of sensory stimulation (touch, sight, sound, and movement). Infants vary in their thresholds for stimulation, and it is one of the tasks of parenthood to try to know one's individual baby well enough to supply his particular needs.

We are living in a period of change and increasing demands for more change, but I feel we should be extremely careful as to how changes in our culture affect our child-rearing practices. Our children will have the best chance of becoming competent adults if we do our job well as parents. They require our help in learning to handle their sexual and aggressive impulses. They need both love and limits from us in ample quantities. Hopefully, they will acquire a sufficient degree of self-esteem to enable them to meet life's challenges. We, as parents, are their first and most important teachers and we should take this responsibility seriously.

I would ask parents to think about some of the propositions put forth in this book, and to utilize the information in keeping with the uniqueness of their own particular child. Our goal should be to help a child make the most of his potential, whatever it may be. For each new human being presents us, as parents, the opportunity to be instrumental in fashioning a work of art.

Bennett Olshaker
Washington, D.C.
October 30, 1974

THE
CHILD
AS A
WORK
OF ART

Chapter I

The Child as a Work of Art

For over twenty-five years I have had the privilege of working with children and parents, first as a pediatrician and later as a child psychiatrist, and during this time, I have watched infants grow up and become young adults. As I look at some of them today, it occurs to me that a young person can truly represent a work of art, and that many parents should be recognized as gifted artists.

Some time ago, I viewed Michelangelo's statue of "David," and I was amazed that anyone could fashion such a lifelike figure from a piece of inert stone. I now wonder if the task of rearing a competent human being, with all the complexities involved, does not require as great a dedication to the chosen art of parenthood.

Not every baby born automatically becomes a work of art. In many instances, children with great potential never utilize very much of it. Yet others, even those with marked limitations in childhood due to physical or mental deficiencies, make the most of what they have. These children are successful because of the care, devotion, and dedication of their parents. Yet the importance of the art of parenthood appears to be constantly downgraded in our culture. We frequently hear in our media that a woman is unfulfilled if all she does is stay home and raise children. I've even encountered women who feel guilty because they really do enjoy being home with their children and looking after their youngsters' needs. They say most of their friends are out working part-time and these acquaintances act as if there is something wrong with a mother who feels her most important function is to be home raising her family.

I have the impression that there are many parents who intuitively realize the value of being with their children and thereby providing the youngsters with the proper beginnings for a good life. However, many of these people begin to doubt the validity of their own feelings when they hear so many others talking of the need for individual fulfillment, which, somehow, has to result from endeavors other than being a good parent.

Those who believe that being a competent parent is of utmost importance should stand by their convictions. On the basis of my observation and experience, there is no more important task. For if we have practiced well the art of parenthood, we will have passed on through our children our feelings and our values. Hopefully, we will have prepared our children to repeat the process in future generations. And I submit that this can provide a greater benefit for humanity than what most of us accomplish in our business or profession. Our offspring ultimately become our greatest and longest-lasting legacy.

Yet so many parents behave as if children are a burden rather than a welcomed obligation. They spend too little time with their youngsters and complain about the time they do spend with them—like an acquaintance of mine who could not wait for her children to go off to summer camp. When I asked her whether she and her husband would take a vacation trip, she reacted as if I'd asked a stupid question. She went on to say that a trip would be unnecessary because she and her husband would just take advantage of the children's absence to enjoy themselves. They would save the trip for the fall or winter when their youngsters would be home and attending school. This would give them another opportunity to get away from the children.

Each of us should do a considerable amount of thinking as to whether or not we should have children. A cartoon I keep on the bulletin board of my waiting room sums up the dilemma nicely. It shows a father looking at a book and saying to his wife, "There's one trouble with these books about raising kids. By the time you're reading them, it's too late not to have any."

No child can decide whether or not to be born. Once here, the infant is completely dependent on his environment for a relatively long time. He cannot survive unless someone cares for him. But how he survives will depend on the quantity and quality of care he receives. He requires that his physical and emotional needs be met. And while he does not ask to be born, he comes equipped with a legitimate due bill for care from his parents.

That bill can be a high one, taxing and testing a couple's maturity to the fullest. A husband may find himself increasingly irritated with his wife after the arrival of a first child— when two rivals are competing for the attention of the mother. A wife who is used to having her own needs met may become greatly irritated by the demands the newly arrived infant makes on her. Therefore, some couples who have gotten along splendidly begin to have marital problems when the requirements of parenthood are placed upon them.

More and more, I have become convinced of the importance of young couples really considering the advisability of becoming parents. We are being faced on many fronts with calls for liberation. Husbands want to be liberated from alimony and child support. Wives want to be liberated from child care. The time has come to decide whether we should have more day care or fewer children. In times past, there was a stigma attached to not having children. Today, however, most couples have a greater freedom of choice. With the exception of those whose deep religious convictions will not allow for contraception or abortion, responsible individuals in this day and age should be able to decide whether or not they want children. In fact, the prevailing attitudes toward ecology and smaller families actually makes the decision not to have children more socially acceptable. Logically, there is no excuse for not thinking out the matter clearly.

Again, no child can ask to be born, but having arrived he should receive all the care, love, and devotion due him. The infant cannot cry for liberation. Children's liberation should consist of not being born to parents who really do not want and who are not prepared to devote the time, energy, and, yes, the sacrifice of a degree of freedom which the rearing of children demands.

If we look about us, we see the results of neglect and actual abuse of youngsters. It runs the gamut from the very obvious battered child to the child suffering from the subtle neglect of a mother who becomes so busy doing good deeds in her community that she turns her own offspring over to the care of others. Traditionally, fathers are most guilty of not spending enough time with their families, but what I fear now is that in the process of seeking their own rights women will be shirking parental responsibility as so many men have done. Rather than having Father there more, we will be having Mother there less. All this will be detrimental to the child's optimal development.

True liberation for husband and wife should include the privilege of not having children. Recently, a husband and wife, both of whom are excellent physicians, told me of their decision not to have any children. They said it was not an easy decision for them to make. They had very mixed feelings about the matter. But they both said they were involved in so many activities they wanted to continue that they felt it would be unfair to have children and then not devote the time it would take to raise them properly. They did not opt for having offspring and putting them in the care of a maid, housekeeper, or day-care center.

When I thought about this couple's decision in light of what might be important to me, I felt perhaps they would be missing something in life without children. However, I admire their decision, and I would hope more people would go through a process of soul-searching in an attempt to determine whether or not they really should have babies.

Instead of such hard decision making, we hear the call for universal day care. It is not that I am entirely against day care. I am against day care being demanded as if it is an inalienable right of each man and woman to have a child and let others care for him while the biological parent does his thing. The "biological parent" conceives the child, but that does not make him a parent in the sense of the ongoing day-to-day process of rearing an adequate person.

Unfortunately, there are parents who must work and leave their children to the care of others. For such people, we do need day-care centers, and we should see to it that such facilities are established with the utmost regard for the rights and well-being of children. We often hear of the need for day-care centers to enable mothers who are on welfare to work.

The implication here is that any paying job is more important than caring for children. In the long run, I believe we would be better off if the welfare mothers were paid and trained to be good mothers to their children rather than to be trained for other employment. The benefits to society ultimately accruing from the better care of these children would far outweigh any short-term gain involved in preparing welfare mothers for other occupations.

What does it take to be a good parent? This is a question I frequently have been asked. My first answer is to be fortunate enough to be born to good parents, for certainly much of our behavior stems from lessons learned before we are even verbal. One could say that our preparation for parenthood starts in our own infancy. The examples set by our parents will have a tremendous effect on the way we will act as parents.

In my work as a child psychiatrist, I hear from parents about their own childhoods. Often, they greatly disliked the way they were handled by their parents but find themselves repeating the same pattern with their youngsters. Or, they react in a pendulumlike fashion and swing to the opposite pole in dealing with their own offspring. So a parent who as a child was punished very harshly may repeat the process with his own child while another parent may be reluctant ever to punish his offspring. Reason would tell us that neither extreme is good. But, of course, often we react with our emotions and not with our reason.

What can individuals do who have not been lucky enough to grow up with good parents? For one thing, they can stop and take a hard look at how they are doing as parents. This involves looking carefully at their youngsters: Are they getting along fairly comfortably with the important ongoing process of their emotional development? Too often, we are burdened with other details of living and do not really look at our children. We do not actually see and hear what is going on. This is especially true if youngsters are quiet and not engaging in troublesome behavior.

An interesting phenomenon frequently occurs in my practice that illustrates how we forget to take notice of our children. Parents will call for an appointment, wanting to come in for psychiatric consultation, in regard to a problem their child is having. At times, because of my busy schedule, they are given an appointment four or five weeks away. When they arrive in my consultation room on the appointed day, I often will hear something like the following, "You know, doctor, since we called you things have improved so much we didn't know whether we should have even kept this appointment."

What has happened? My own feeling is that, having come to the point of making an appointment with the psychiatrist, the parents have at least accepted the fact that something is not going well. The stimulus for such an action may have come from the school or some other agent outside the immediate family, but once the parents are motivated sufficiently to make the appointment, they begin to observe their child's behavior and their own more closely. Once this observation process has begun, they are probably more conscious of what they and their child have been doing. Then things do begin to change and, by the time they keep their appointment, the situation has improved.

In order to be better parents, then, we need to practice self-observation in relationship to our children's behavior and not just be bothered by their behavior. When self-scrutiny does not seem to work, we may have to turn for additional evaluation and help to various disciplines involved in the diagnosis and treatment of parent-child problems.

But no matter what else is involved, one of the most important elements in being a good parent is the *desire* to be one, and the willingness to commit one's self to practicing the art of parenthood. This art is a difficult one, for a child is not a piece of clay, but an infinitely complex, always changing individual. And no two children are alike. Some are blessed with an ability to withstand a great deal of emotional trauma, while others are more adversely affected by what might seem like relatively minimal psychological injury. Infants also vary in their constitutional make-up. Some possess certain talents which others do not. Some have physical problems while others do not.

While we should not think of a child as raw material to be converted into an object of our choosing, we should think of him as something valuable—something to be nurtured and helped to make the most of his endowments. This makes me think of how foolish it sounds when people refer to their children as "jewels" or "treasures." Why should we compare our most valuable possessions, namely our offspring, to pieces of stone? In truth, a good human being should be the standard by which to judge value.

When I see a young adult who is able to function well no matter what his original assets or liabilities, I consider him to be truly a work of art. The standard I apply is not one of specific perfection or accomplishment. We all know of men of genius who are failures in the realm of warm and loving interchange with their fellow-men. To me, the young adult who approaches what I conceive of as a work of art is the individual who is productive, has a sufficient degree of self-esteem, can care for and be concerned about others, and in general, is comfortable with himself. I do not feel that this just happens. I believe it is the result of dedication on the part of parents.

I was once asked during a television interview, "Aren't there too many books being written with advice for parents?

Doesn't this get confusing?'' This was a difficult question to answer, for it is understandable that parents may get confused when they read diametrically opposite advice on child rearing given by two ''experts.'' Again, if each child is unique, how can such advice help? And how reliable are the experts?

The only advantage we so-called experts have is that we have had the opportunity to study human growth and development over a long period of time and to see a large number of families and children. I do not believe we can give parents exact formulas that will work for every situation. But I have great faith in the ability of parents to look carefully at what they and their children are doing. Let them note whether or not the information they read seems to make sense and if it can be used to advantage in their particular circumstances. If not, they might be better off to ignore it.

In the chapters that follow, I will be setting down some of my views on what is required to guide a child through infancy to competent young adulthood. These opinions are based on my experience in the fields of pediatrics and psychiatry. Some might agree with my opinions, others might disagree. There are no exact rules for success here, because there are none. I feel that the proper raising of children is an art at which we as parents will be successful to varying degrees. I do not put my faith in formulas, but rather in the ability of people who really want to be parents.

Chapter II

Changing Attitudes Toward Women

In examining the subject of proper child care, I find myself becoming increasingly concerned about the unrest and dissatisfaction among women in our culture. Although we are primarily interested here in the needs and rights of children, I nevertheless feel that we cannot afford to overlook the many complaints of the Women's Movement.

Perhaps my personal experience with women's liberation will illustrate what I mean. Until recently, I genuinely felt the charge of male chauvinism could not be leveled at me. I saw myself as a relatively good husband and father, who had benefited not only from raising three children, but also from twenty-five years of pediatrics and child psychiatry. In keeping with my "available time," I had helped with household chores and child-care duties. With a certain amount of pride, I looked at a photograph of myself bathing my first son and thought, "Well, most fathers would not be involved in something like that." I was aware that fathers should spend time with children, and I patted myself on the back for doing so— especially when it was time I could have spent on my career.

I remember how, at the age of twelve, one of my sons asked, "Dad, could you be a famous psychiatrist?" After about thirty seconds, I answered.

"Yes, I guess I could. I'm probably as smart as most of the other doctors and more creative than some, but I'll tell you what I'd have to do. I'd have to write more papers, go to more meetings, more conventions, take part in more community activities. And if I did that, I would not have as much time to spend at home with you, your brothers, and Mom."

After hearing this, my son said, "Well, you don't have to be famous."

When the children were older, I did not object to my wife's going back to school, and I was happy when she accepted a part-time job. I knew she was an intelligent, talented person who had had to give up a good deal to raise her children. I also knew she considered the children to be of primary importance, and that I had helped out when I could. And so I went along without any further examination of my own ideas.

One evening not too long ago, however, I was surprised by a discussion I had with my wife about child care. As we spoke, she came up with some thoughts and questions which rocked my complacency and forced me to face questions which had never bothered me before.

"You know that I feel taking care of kids is very important," she said, "but did you ever think to ask me before we had children or during all those years they were growing up just how I felt about being at home with them all the time, and how I felt about giving up other opportunities? Did you ever wonder how I was coping with any aggressive drives I had, or the resentment I might have over not being able to choose whether or not I wanted to stay home and take care of children?

"Do you know any husbands who were concerned with what their wives were giving up? Who were concerned with what their wives wanted to do? Who questioned them about what they planned to do when the children were older?"

My first response was an attempt to justify my position. "I never objected to your doing what you wanted," I said. "I may not have had a positive attitude toward what you were experiencing, but at least I wasn't negative—which is more than I can say for a lot of husbands."

"That's just it," she replied. "You weren't involved. Maybe if you had objected, I would have felt you were aware of my feelings."

"But no other husbands of our generation thought about those things."

"That is exactly my point. No one cared that women had no choice. It was just assumed that this was what they had to do. Some women probably were not even aware of their resentment, but the anger and frustration were there just the same. Perhaps it was necessary for wives to stay home and take care of the kids because the husband could make more money—but none of you thought to ask us how we felt about it. There is a tremendous amount of resentment among women. Even the woman who wants to stay home with her children feels that what she is doing is taken for granted. She thinks it is all simply expected of her, and she's angry about it. This is really what so much of the women's revolution is all about."

It wasn't easy for me to think back over our twenty-eight years of marriage and have to admit that what my wife said was really true. It is simple and requires little insight to say, "Yes, women should certainly be entitled to equal pay for equal work and equal opportunity for employment." But it is not quite so easy for us to look at ourselves and question our own attitudes.

What my wife was concerned about was the woman's lack of freedom and the man's lack of understanding that while they have a choice, women do not. Even the mother who wants to care for her children and does it well may resent children, because it is not something she does freely and willingly. It is something that is expected of her.

When a woman feels that no one values what she is doing, she finds it difficult to value herself. This is why I encounter so many women who resist the idea that caring for children is a most significant job or an art. These women maintain that anyone can take care of children. In order to fulfill themselves, they feel they must get a job and make money. Only earning power can prove their worth and productivity.

As a psychiatrist interested in the welfare of children, I am worried by this way of thinking. The children's welfare may be adversely affected—even if the most excellent day care is available.

What can we do? I think one solution is to look at the family as a cooperative enterprise. In today's society, men are able to earn more money than their wives. Leaving aside the question of whether or not this is as it should be, I would advocate the following: In each family in which the husband earns the livelihood and the wife has primary responsibility for the children, the wife's contribution should be considered equal to her husband's. She is therefore earning half the family's income. She should not have to depend on her husband's generosity for an allowance or have to degrade herself by asking for money, since half of what they have is rightfully hers.

The day may yet come when fathers and mothers will

share equally in child care and household duties. For the present, however, we must look at what is, and has been going on—and that is that most of our children are taken care of by their mothers.

Although I am sensitive to the feelings of today's women, this does not affect at all my deep conviction that a child deserves all the love, care, and devotion necessary for his or her optimal growth and development. In the future, we need to put more emphasis on how the father can be more involved, but for now, we must be careful not to abruptly make changes in our methods of caring for children that may prove to be undesirable.

We must continue to ask some important questions. For example, is there a biological or natural basis for a primary attachment between an infant and its mother? Studies with primates other than man would indicate that such an attachment does exist. There are those who feel the same is true for human infants. My own feeling is that—certainly during the first year of life—a primary relationship to an interested and involved mother is the best situation for an infant.

This, of course, does not mean that we men are out of the child-raising picture. If we can't play as active a role as our wives, we can try to understand our spouses' experience. Consider, for example, that when it comes to the raising of children, the satisfaction does not come immediately upon completion of good work, as it often does in a man's occupational work. In parenthood, there are no immediate victories and, consequently, no adequate standard to measure day-to-day accomplishment. Certainly a child's smile or hug can be rewarding, but if a mother measures her worth in terms of how well she does her job, she will have to wait a long time before she can see how the finished product turns out.

In addition, a mother has relatively little control over a

complex of variables—such as the child's temperament, illnesses, the community and school situation, or even her own and her husband's personalities. Yet she is often blamed for whatever goes wrong. Her husband may complain if the children make too much noise when he comes home from a hard day's work. The school criticizes her if the child has not done his homework or is misbehaving. Grandparents may complain that she is not raising the child properly. Everyone blames her, and too often, she blames herself even when she is doing a good job.

All this brings us back to the question of what we males should be thinking and doing in relation to these problems. Trying to understand our wives' feelings and problems is one step in the right direction. Another crucial factor is giving thought to the dilemma of what the woman will do when the children no longer require as much of her time and mothering. My wife recently commented to me that many men are putting aside money and expressing concern over the future education of their children, but they do not seem to concern themselves with the future education or vocation of their wives.

We must think about what a woman will be able to do once the children are grown. Thought must be given to establish a setup for part-time work during the children's school years, to later refresher courses, supplemental training, and placement. Even the skills learned and employed in the process of raising children go to waste. When one sees the poor state of nursing care in many of our hospitals, it seems only natural that some of our middle-aged mothers, who now have worked themselves out of their primary jobs, could receive nursing training and help improve the hospital situation.

Most of us who are veterans of the armed forces have benefited from provisions of the G.I. Bill in securing further education. Why shouldn't veterans of motherhood be afforded the opportunity to be trained or retrained for satisfying work of their choosing?

Unfortunately, the woman who wants to do this often runs into all sorts of opposition. Recently I read about a fifty-two-year-old grandmother who tried to enroll in medical school. At first she was told repeatedly that her age was against her. Enrollment spaces were limited and she could not take the place of a twenty-two-year-old student who would practice many more years. Statistically, there may be some validity to this argument, but we need to look at these matters in a broader framework. This woman, who finally was allowed to enroll and who graduated with distinction, will probably practice for about twenty years. Society will be well repaid for whatever part of her education it supplied. In addition to the technical skills she learned, she can bring the wisdom, insight, and compassion developed during her years of motherhood and grandmotherhood, qualities too often lacking in some of the brilliant younger men and women who can withstand the current competition for the available medical school admissions.

The question of quotas for school admission is always a touchy one, but I believe we need to reorient ourselves to provide opportunities to the women who have decided to spend part of their lives at the important task of raising children. Regrettably, even those who try cannot often succeed as did the grandmother who went to medical school. Increasingly, medical and law schools and other professional institutions arbitrarily eliminate applicants on the basis of standardized tests, with little or no regard for the many other qualities a person might be able to contribute. And being an older female creates additional barriers to further education and training. I mention law and medical school because the admissions problem is clear-cut and easy to grasp, but analogous situations exist in a multitude of fields where the acceptance criteria are so narrow as to exclude all but one specific type. Not only does this ultimately damage the particular field of study and practice, it is a further example of the type of rigid cultural patterns which serve not the ongoing needs of the society, but the status quo.

One might conclude from all this that I am more concerned with the care of mothers than the care of children. My point is simply that, if we are going to have the best possible care for our children, we will have to deal with the feelings and problems of their primary caretakers—and thereby add new dimensions to the art of parenthood.

Chapter III

Who Should Care for Our Children?

Who should care for our children? This is a more complicated question than it looks and, inevitably, gives rise to other questions. What, for example, are the effects on a child's development if a mother works outside the home? What are the effects if a mother is unhappy about having to stay home all day? If a mother does work, what are the optimal arrangements for the care of the child? Does the child's age make any difference in what type of care should be provided? Where should fathers fit into the picture?

We could go on and on posing questions. The fact is the problem of child care is multifaceted. Furthermore, where humans are involved, it is extremely difficult (and often impossible) to set up controlled studies of the effects of one type of handling as compared with another.

My own point of view regarding the best possible child care represents an amalgam of my own experience, reading, professional training, observations, and discussions with others. I do believe that within the realm of child care there is much room for differences of opinion and various possible alternatives. We should realize that individual children will require different types of handling. What is the optimal care situation for one may not be what is best for another.

Some basics of child care are universal. For one thing, the attachment of the infant to other human beings is important. For another, an infant requires consistent and sensitive care in as stable an environment as possible, free from severe nutritional and physical deprivations. The question which remains is how this care can best be given and by whom.

I do feel there can be substitutes for the mother. In fact, circumstances make it necessary at times: for example, when an infant is orphaned or when a mother abandons her infant and the father or someone else must care for the baby.

One trend in child rearing I definitely feel to be positive is the increased involvement of fathers. I believe that the individual newborn is entitled to the best "parenting" he or she can have—and this includes both parents. Fathers should be involved from the beginning and to a greater extent than they have been in the past.

One positive aspect of this trend is that, increasingly, fathers are being admitted to the delivery room so that they can be part of the infant's life from the beginning. A local pediatrician told me that, in the hospital where he practices, about thirty to forty per cent of the fathers were availing themselves of this opportunity. I cannot imagine that this will have anything but a salutary effect on the feelings of these men toward their newborn children.

Yes, fathers can and should be more involved in the care of their infants. How much more will depend on the individual background, orientation, and life style of a particular couple. No matter what the experts say, each pair of parents will ultimately decide for themselves how they will raise their child. What each couple can and should do, I think, is to look at the information available to guide them in choosing between various child-care alternatives. My feeling is that until or unless proven otherwise, there are strong factors which favor the view that a mother is the best choice as a primary caretaker of the infant, especially during the first two years of life.

It is she, after all, who carries the fetus within her body during the nine months of pregnancy. She undergoes physical, hormonal, and psychological changes as she feels the baby moving within her body. Interestingly, infants who were unplanned or perhaps even unwanted often become more accepted during this period. By the time the child is born, the mother has undergone experiences which prepare her for attachment to her baby.

The type of delivery a mother experiences may affect the bonding process between her and her offspring. A mother who is awake and can see and touch her baby soon after birth may feel closer to the infant than a mother who has had a great deal of anesthesia and is not awake at the time of delivery or shortly thereafter. The infant whose mother had been heavily anesthetized may react more sluggishly for some time after its birth.

Studies have shown that sustained contact between mother and infant in the period following delivery is also important for both. Of course, we do not set up experiments in humans in which we deliberately cause separation. But there are instances where existing conditions have enabled investigators to study the effects of maternal-infant separation. Dr. Clicord Barnett and associates of the Stanford University School of Medicine conducted a two-year study involving mothers of premature infants. Because of the low birth weight and physical immaturity of the newborn premature infant, its mother is generally deprived of any contact with the baby other than perhaps viewing him through the window of the nursery. Usually, they are without physical contact until the third to twelfth week after delivery. In the Stanford study, however, forty-one mothers were permitted to handle and later feed their infants in the premature nursery. Thirteen mothers from this group were selected at random for observation and interview during the time their infants were in the nursery and after discharge. A group of sixteen mothers who were not permitted to enter the nursery to tend their babies was also studied.

While the authors of this study state that many variables besides separation may affect the mother's interaction with her child, they concluded that "on a case basis, differences between those mothers who were allowed into the nursery and experienced only partial interactional deprivation and those who were not allowed in and thus underwent a longer period of severe deprivation appeared to center in three areas: commitment to the infant, self-confidence in the ability to mother the infant, and behavior toward the infant (e.g. stimulation and skill in caretaking)." In all three areas, mothers who had been in closest contact with their premature babies tended to display the most positive interactional behavior.

In earlier times, mothers often delivered their infants at home and there was substantially less separation between them and their babies than we now have. In most conventional hospitals, the infant remains in a special nursery and is only brought to the mother at specified times.

At the Case Western Reserve School of Medicine, Dr. Marshall Klaus and his coworkers compared two groups of mothers, fourteen women in each group. All were having their first baby and all had normal full-term deliveries. In one group, the normal hospital routine was followed. Each mother was given a glimpse of her baby at birth and a brief contact six to twelve hours later. Following this, she had the baby for twenty to thirty minutes during feeding time every four hours.

The second group was given what was termed "extended contact" with their infants. Within the first three hours after birth, they were given their nude babies with a heat panel overhead. They were allowed to keep them for a period of one hour. Also, for the first three days after delivery, they had five extra hours of contact with the babies each afternoon. All of the babies in both groups were being bottle-fed. All the mothers were studied twenty-eight to thirty-two days later by means of a standardized interview, examination of the baby, and a filmed bottle-feeding. It was noted that in the extended contact group, each mother was more reluctant to leave her baby with someone else. They usually stood and watched during the examination of the baby, they showed greater soothing behavior and they engaged in significantly more eye-to-eye contact and fondling.

While the aforementioned studies involve relatively small numbers of cases, they do suggest that some of our current hospital practices may interfere with the development of beneficial relationships between parents and infants.

Some hospitals have instituted what is called "rooming in." In this situation, the baby is kept in a bassinet near the mother's bed rather than in the conventional newborn nursery. Mothers in rooming in setups are encouraged to care for their own babies as soon as they are able. M. Greenberg and associates, in a study conducted in Sweden, compared two groups of fifty mothers each who were assigned at random to either rooming in or a conventional obstetrical-nursery setting. Again, all the mothers were having a first child and the two groups were similar in terms of age, socioeconomic characteristics, and the age and education of their husbands. The rooming in mothers had the babies in their rooms from 9 a.m. to 6 p.m. while, in the conventional setting, each baby was only in the mother's room for twenty minutes at each feeding. Both groups fed their babies on a regular schedule. The results of this study concluded that the ". . . rooming in mothers judged themselves to be more confident and competent in baby care, thought they would need less help in caring for their infants at home, and could attribute more to their babies' cries than the nonrooming in mothers." Other studies have shown that increased contact between mother and infant in the hospital can lead to greater confidence in the mother.

Once home from the hospital, close contact should continue. In many middle- and upper-class households, practical nurses are hired to care for the infants during the first few weeks after delivery to give the mother a rest. In other instances, an outside relative may be brought in to serve the same function. Most often, the nurse or relative will feed the baby, sparing the mother the "trouble" and thereby permitting her to take it easy for the first few weeks. I feel that we really need to consider the advisability of such a practice because more physical contact between mother and infant during these early days can be a positive factor in later relationships. It would be better to have the helper do everything around the home except care for the baby and permit the mother and child to have as much time and contact with each other as possible.

When I review all the information available to us today, then I conclude that the mother is the best caretaker for the child, particularly during its infancy. This is especially true when the mother genuinely wants to devote herself to this task. The father should also be increasingly involved, however, so that attachment develops between him and the baby as well. As I have said, there are cases where surrogate mothers are necessary, but all things being equal, there is no substitute for a child's own parents, especially his mother.

Realistically, of course, we must recognize that many mothers do work. In 1973, according to the Women's Bureau of the U.S. Department of Labor, there were 13.6 million employed mothers in the U.S. Forty-three per cent of all mothers of children eighteen years of age and younger were employed outside the home. Three and four-tenths million employed mothers are single parents and the only income-producing adult in their families. In many families the father is unable to earn sufficient money and the mother must work to maintain the family's financial stability. Other mothers work out of choice to maintain a career or simply because they enjoy working more than staying at home.

We often hear talk of the possibility of a four-day work week instead of the conventional five-day week. Perhaps we should begin thinking rather of a five-hour work day so designed that mothers and fathers who both work could have different shifts, freeing each to be available for child care, particularly during their youngsters' preschool years.

While it is difficult for me to believe that any caretaker is better for a child than his own interested parents, I nevertheless recognize that there are conflicts between the child's needs and the parents' needs. Also, there are often conflicts between the child's needs and the reality imposed by the death of a parent, separation and divorce, or economic hardship. Therefore, we must consider what type of care can be provided when the parents are unavailable.

Recognizing the need for surrogate caretakers in some cases is one thing—but this should not be used as proof of the necessity for universal day care. We need to be extremely careful regarding what we do out of choice and what we must do out of necessity. I strongly feel that some of the all-out advocates of day care are offering pie-in-the-sky solutions to parents. For example, an article I read recently about how adequate day care ought to be organized gave me the feeling that to accomplish these objectives would require super-parent-surrogates.

The article, by Christoph Heinicke and the American Orthopsychiatric Association Study Group on the Mental Health Aspects of Day Care, stated: "In summary, our developmental criteria for the evaluation of day care programs stress attention to individual needs, attention to all areas of functioning . . . promotion of the child's active choice in what he does and learns, encouragement in learning to deal with a variety of feelings, and enhancement of the quality of engagement as opposed to passive receiving."

To produce this kind of care would be tremendously expensive. It would require both excellently trained personnel and, to be of value to children, continuity of personnel. Dr. Dale Meers of the Children's Hospital National Medical Center of Washington, D.C., in testimony before the U.S. Senate Subcommittee on Children and Youth Concerning Day Care Legislation, March 27, 1972, stated, "All child care programs that I know of internationally, including those of the kibbutzim, have had chronic problems in obtaining and keeping appropriate staff." He adds that ". . . day care is expensive if it is to be organized and directed effectively." He commented in his testimony that ". . . effective day care is urgently needed today—as a remedial program that with all its limitations, is undoubtedly better than the neglect of our most disadvantaged children." But he also made the point that it should be restricted to demonstration projects until the programs and psychiatric evaluations of their effects could be studied.

There is no doubt that in many disadvantaged families a

good type of day care may be helpful and important in trying to undo the damage of deprivation. Even with these families, a better solution might be parent-child day centers where welfare mothers could be helped to become more adequate parents. This might be a positive function rather than simply having the center provide care for the children so that the mothers can become part of the work force.

Where group day care is not a necessity, we should think twice about its value. Proponents of group day care often point to some of the Socialist countries as being ahead of us in the provision of day-care facilities. Dr. Marie Meierhofer, director of the Institute for Psychohygiene in Adolescents at Zürich, found substantial depression in many of the infants she studied in Europe. She felt that the countries in which children were put into nurseries at an early age while their mothers worked were beginning to see the errors of their system of child care. In a recent study in Hungary, she noted that mothers there can now draw wages for a year or more after the birth of a baby while staying at home and caring for the young child. And Dr. Meers, in his testimony before the U.S. Senate, noted that the research on the distress of young children in day care had persuaded Czechoslovakia to reverse its national policy and that that country was now actively dissuading its citizens, by national TV, from placing children under the age of three in day care centers.

In his own study and observations of Communist centers, Meers was depressed by the large number of passive and despondent children that he saw. He feels that to have effective day care, ratios of adults to children must be kept very low.

Some of the proponents of group day care base their recommendations on studies of demonstration projects. Considerable thought, effort, professionalism, and money has been put into these projects. It is probably unreasonable to expect that the majority of day-care centers would be run in such a fashion once the program was widespread. Even if the necessary funds were available, one wonders where we would get a staff who could supply to infants and children what they should reasonably expect from their parents.

I realize that I approach the subject of day care with a certain ambivalence. I feel that it is best for children to have their needs met by their own parents, although, even when a mother, or in some cases these days, a father, remains at home, he or she is not always able (or willing) to actually devote the time to the child. Being at home all day with a child can be boring—and some families who can afford it put their children in nursery schools for part of the day when they reach the age of three or four. I would certainly want to see children below the age of two at home with their mother or father, but even with this age group there are mothers who must work. Again, each family must make up its own mind as to what arrangements are to be made for their children, but the matter should be given considerable thought—particularly with young infants.

So far I have spoken mainly of group day care. Actually, there are alternatives. Many children of working parents are cared for in what is referred to as family day care. This is a private home in which a woman (or, less often, a man) cares for one or more children during the day. Dr. Arthur C. Emlen, Professor of Social Work at Portland State University and Project Director of the Field Study of the Neighborhood Family Day Care System in Portland, Oregon, has found that a great number of women prefer this type of situation. Not only is it more convenient, flexible, and controllable than group day care, but it also generally provides a more comfortable and familiar setting with the kind of responsible support, comfort, love, and learning experiences that the child needs. He feels, "It is a form of care that probably offers less risk of abuse, exploitation or custodial deprivation than commercial care and large group care programs." Emlen concludes that while private family day care ranges from excellent to bad, most is satisfactory and it is a significant resource for good day care in the United States.

In another study relating to family day care, June Solnit Sale, of the Community Day Care Project, Pacific Oaks College, Pasadena, California, found that the ". . . key to quality had to do with the family day-care mother herself." She felt that this form of day care has a great deal to offer, particularly when it is set up as a self-help organization in which the "mothers" work together ". . . to improve family day care for the children, their families, and the day-care mothers themselves." There may be an entire group of older people who could function as substitute mothers or grandmothers, and this could, perhaps, be developed into a useful and necessary occupation.

Many families arrange for in-home care with a maid or housekeeper to tend the child or children. Here again, the type of care depends on the quality of the person giving the care.

If parents are not careful in selecting a substitute, they invite difficulties—and in some cases, disaster. I remember, several years ago, getting a call from the children of an acquaintance of mine. The parents had gone on a trip and left the children with a maid they had hired less than a week before they left. The children called because the maid was drunk and had passed out.

I am constantly amazed when I return parents' calls to find that the phone is answered by household help who cannot understand English. These individuals are left alone to care for young infants and children. Fortunately, emergencies are rare—but they do occur. One wonders what a person without knowledge of our language would be able to do in such a situation.

Parents also are sometimes careless in choosing summer camps for their children. I have seen numerous cases of children being sent off to a camp where the care and supervision turned out to be substandard or, in a few cases, downright negligent. I have known of children who undergo traumatic experiences with other campers or even maladjusted counselors and are afraid to tell their parents about it. It should be incumbent on each of us to make sure that the people to whom we entrust our children in any situation are competent and reliable.

Hopefully, however, parents will remain the principal caretakers for their own children whenever possible. This brings me again to what I feel is a very important point—more people should decide not to have children rather than to neglect them once they are born.

In summary, I feel that during the first two years of life, the infant will benefit most from a close relationship with his parents, especially his mother. After this period, the child still needs continuing care. He needs to be comfortable in the knowledge that his mother and father will not be absent for prolonged periods of time. If we pay more attention to the establishment of the proper bonds between parents and child in the earliest hours and days of life, we will probably have more parents who really care and want to care for their children.

Chapter IV

The Importance of Infancy

Just as the foundation of a building is essential to the soundness of the structure, so are the early experiences of an infant crucial to the development of the person he grows up to be. I am convinced that if we are to aim toward the objective of having each human being make the most of his or her potential throughout life, we must pay increasing attention to what goes on during the earliest part of that life—especially the first year.

Everyone realizes that in order to survive, the human infant must have his physical needs met. When he comes into the world, he is a totally dependent organism. It takes him nine months to develop within his mother's body, and it usually takes another nine months before he even has the physical ability to crawl away from his mother. He must be fed, kept warm, and protected from a wide variety of dangers.

But in order to thrive (and, in some instances, to survive), the infant needs more than to have his nutritional needs supplied. Beginning at birth, he needs an adequate measure of sensory stimulation. While there is still much to be learned about the effects of inadequate or overly intense sensory stimulation, there is already ample evidence that the lack of sufficient physical contact and tenderness can be extremely detrimental to the infant's optimal development.

Almost thirty years ago, Dr. René Spitz observed the adverse effects of long-term maternal separation upon an infant's development. Infants cared for in a foundling home, where only their basic physical needs were met, became depressed and their physical development tended to be subnormal. Another group of infants was studied, whose mothers were in an institution for delinquent girls, while the infants were kept for most of the time in a nursery. This group of babies were cared for part of the time, however, by their own mothers. They fared much better and did not show the same signs of depression and ill health as the babies from the foundling home. As we can see, the one important difference between the two groups was the individual care and sensory stimulation they received.

Anyone involved in pediatrics and psychiatry will recognize, from his own clinical experience, the importance of the human infant having a close, dependable, loving relationship with a "caretaking" person. The baby needs such a relationship in order to be able to develop the capacity for attachment to others later on. While some object that most studies focus on the early relationship between mother and child and don't pay attention to fathers or other possible primary caretakers for the newborn, I feel we should focus on mothers. There must be some wisdom in nature's providing mothers with the biological capacity to carry the infant before birth and to feed it from her own body after delivery.

While in the first few months of life the infant must receive adequate stimulation, he probably does not connect this spe-

cifically with the person of his mother. By approximately
four months of age, he develops an awareness of himself as a
dependent part of another person. He begins to learn about
closeness and attachment. Soon, when he begins to crawl, he
will show evidence of anxiety due to fear of separation from
the person on whom he has come to depend. As his capacity
for attachment to his mother continues to grow, the baby also
develops a greater ability to become attached to others.

Many observations have been made in regard to infant-
mother interactions. But one obviously cannot set up experimental conditions to purposely study the effects of deprivation or substitution of a mother or surrogate mother. However, a great deal can be done in the study of animal
primates, and the findings are worth thinking about. Dr.
Harry F. Harlow, for example, has conducted a great many
experiments, using rhesus monkeys as his subjects. He feels
that "during the first year of life there is a close similarity in
the behavior patterns of monkey and child and in the developmental stages through which they go. This is not only true
for affection, but it also holds for such emotional patterns as
fear and anger and even for intellectual growth."

Harlow's work with rhesus monkeys is interesting to us
because it tells us a great deal about the need for sensory experience and the importance of "contact-comfort." He separated infant monkeys from their mothers at birth and put each
one into a cage with two cubicles. In one cubicle there was a
surrogate mother constructed of wire with no covering. In the
other cubicle was a surrogate mother with a wire frame covered with terry cloth. The monkeys in one group of four were
nursed only from the wire surrogates, while the other four
nursed only from the cloth surrogates. The monkeys had
access to a mother of either type except for the nursing variable. Harlow found that the infants spent from fifteen to

seventeen hours a day with their cloth mothers regardless of which type of mother they actually nursed from. Those who nursed from the wire mothers did not spend more than one or two hours a day with "her." This experiment demonstrated that the infants' attachment developed more through the comfort of contact than through the nursing process.

Harlow's experiments also show that, during the first 150 to 180 days of life, rocking motion is an important variable in the stimulation of infant monkeys. The study goes on to disclose, however, that while nursing and rocking are significant at certain stages of development, they do not provide the long-term attachment of the contact-comfort derived from the cloth mothers. After 180 days, the baby monkeys were separated from their surrogate mothers. They were then tested at periodic intervals for a year and a half afterward. The tests revealed that the period of separation did not destroy the affectional attachment.

Harlow and his associates conducted other experiments along these lines. They discovered, for example, that when confronted with a frightening situation, infant monkeys derived a sense of security from attaching themselves to the cloth surrogate mother. In discussing these findings, Harlow writes: "It is comforting to know that mother love, once formed, apparently remains. Mothers should be cheered when their babies are kicking them on their shins, telling them that they do not love them, or stating that they wish they were dead, to know that the infant is hopelessly trapped. No matter what he does or says and no matter how little he understands it, the infant belongs to the mother forever, insofar as the primary primate affectional bonds are concerned."

While there may be strong similarities between man and monkey, there are also many differences which must be taken into account. The ethologist Jane Goodall, famous for her studies of man's closest living relative, the chimpanzee, notes that man questions the reasons for his existence and how he came to be the way he is. He tries to understand his own behavior, the world, and the universe. And there is nothing in the rest of the primate world, she notes, to compare with the attributes that ". . . mark human heterosexual love in its highest form." But she also says that, "Man, with his tremendous capacity to love, has a capacity to hate far transcending the worst of the squabbles that may break out between chimpanzees."

It is certainly true that man can make many modifications in his culture and in his child-rearing practices, but the evidence gathered from animal studies seems to tie in quite well with what is observed clinically in human infants. In Goodall's study, she describes the abnormal behavior in three chimpanzees, ages three to four years, who lost their mothers. Two were "adopted" by elder siblings. In spite of this, they became listless and during the first few months, showed declining frequency of play. The behavior of one became extremely abnormal. He finally died of a paralytic disease but was so emaciated that Goodall felt he would have died anyway. A picture of this animal shows an unhappy, withdrawn, depressed look which is very similar to that seen in a depressed infant or child. The third chimpanzee infant, who was not adopted, became lethargic and stopped playing almost entirely. She was presumed dead when, two months after her mother's death, she stopped coming to the feeding area.

The chimpanzee offspring is usually not weaned until the fifth or sixth year, and he is dependent on his mother for several more years—until he reaches sexual maturity. In the final stages of weaning, the young chimpanzee may go through a period of depression. He may be listless and apathetic. His play may decrease and he may cling to his mother as he did earlier in infancy.

Touch is another area in which chimpanzees show many notable similarities to man. The animals may hold hands, touch and pat each other, embrace, kiss, tickle each other with their hair. A frightened adult chimp may reach out to touch or embrace another who happens to be nearby, and this physical contact often calms down the frightened animal.

Various types of sensory stimulation are important to the human infant and, certainly, touch is one of them. Ashley Montagu has devoted a book, *Touching, the Human Significance of the Skin,* to this subject. He has gathered together for the volume evidence from many sources to make his point "that the human significance of touching is considerably more profound than has hitherto been understood. The skin as the sensory receptor organ which responds to contact with the sensation of touch, a sensation to which basic human meanings become attached almost from the moment of birth, is fundamental in the development of behavior."

Ethologists have observed and described characteristics and species-specific maternal behavior in nonhuman mammals. Only relatively recently have investigators begun to explore human maternal behavior. Dr. Marshall Klaus and his associates at Case Western Reserve University studied and recorded the first postnatal contact of twelve mothers of normal full-term infants and nine mothers of premature infants. With the full-term infants, observations were made of the first contact and recorded on film one half hour to thirteen and a half hours following delivery. The mothers of the premature infants were observed during their first three tactile contacts with their infants in incubators. When a mother first saw her newborn baby, an orderly and predictable pattern of behavior was observed. The findings were summarized as follows:

1. Human mothers of full-term infants have an orderly and predictable pattern of behavior when presented with their nude infants shortly after birth. Starting with fingertip touch on the infants' extremities, they proceed in four to eight minutes to massaging, encompassing, and palm contact on the trunk.
2. In mothers of healthy premature infants cared for in incubators, this sequence was altered. (They followed a similar sequence but at a much slower rate.)
3. Early mother-to-infant eye-to-eye contact appears to be a significant interaction during the development of maternal affectional ties.

While this study is of the mother's reaction, it indicates there may be some built-in mechanisms for the beginning stimulation of the infant through tactile and visual senses.

The human infant must accomplish a great deal during his first year and a half. After birth, he enters a period where his brain will grow more rapidly for eighteen or so months than it will during the rest of his lifetime. Dr. Reginald Lourie, of Washington's Children Hospital and George Washington University Medical School, wrote an article concerning the importance of the first three years of life. In it, he states that information is becoming available from work with animals and human infants, which indicates the importance of sensory stimulation in enabling the infant to make the most of the inborn capacities of his brain and nervous system. He quotes

Dr. Humberto Nagera, of the University of Michigan's Child Psychiatric Hospital, as pointing out:

1. The genetic potential, in terms of the development of the anatomical structures of the brain, is not reached at birth. Many such structures are, in fact, far from complete at such a time.

2. The blueprint of that genetic potential (determined by the chromosomes and genes) is such that in order to be unfolded to its fullest, organic, anatomical-maturational processes of the brain structure must continue after birth. But such continuation is not only dependent on internal embryological maturational forces, but . . . in the interaction of such forces with different forms of external stimulation without which interaction the embryological maturational blueprint will not unfold to its fullest potential. Reception of such stimuli, as contained in the ministrations of the mother to her baby, in the mother-child relationship, seems absolutely necessary.

Others have shown that the sensory systems require sensory input during the formative periods of development. Studies in animals have shown that there are differences in the structure and blood supply of parts of the brain when animals are deprived of adequate stimulation. Dr. James Prescott, of the National Institute of Child Health and Human Development, has proposed a theory suggesting that a part of the brain, the cerebellum, becomes supersensitive and overexcitable in its function due to insufficient somatosensory stimulation during early development. He feels that this is an operative factor in the development of socioemotional disor-

ders, particularly pathologic violent behaviors. These are behaviors which may stem from what has been called maternal-
social deprivation.

There are many theories which attempt to explain what ex-
perimenters have noted as the effects of maternal deprivation
in mammals other than man, as well as in man himself.
While they may vary in their opinions as to whether touch or
movement or visual stimuli are most important, there seems
to be general agreement as to the importance of stimulation
and the ill effects of its absence.

What does all of this mean to us in terms of the individual
human infant? It accentuates the importance of the first years
of life. It cautions us to be particularly aware of what we are
doing with infants during this period. In studies of lower
animals, there has been talk of "critical periods" as far as
certain developmental tasks are concerned. In regard to the
human infant, we probably should not think of critical
periods so much as "optimal" periods when certain things
should occur in development. The human infant who does
not receive sufficient stimulation shows lags in his development and may never completely make up for this deficit.

Evidence of this fact was presented by the Swiss child psychiatrist, Dr. Marie Meierhofer, in an interview published in
the *Medical Tribune,* April 5, 1972. She stated that a trained
observer could recognize depression in infants no more than
three months of age. In order to learn to identify depression
rapidly and accurately she filmed five hundred babies who
had been placed in Zurich nurseries by working mothers. The
depressed infants tended to show a low level of activity, apparent apathy, and a typical expression of compressed lips,
and oftentimes, a wrinkled forehead. The babies frequently
cried and covered their eyes when approached.

Dr. Meierhofer feels that such depression is caused by

isolation, which may be due to physical separation from the mother, but may also be due to the fact that the baby is not getting the warm contact from a mother who is with him a good bit of the time. She feels that up to six or seven months, infants can be pulled through an episode of depression in a short time, but as they approach two years of age, they may be in danger of remaining in a depressed state for an extended period. When a child remains in such a state, his normal development may be arrested and he may show abnormalities in his speech, motor activity, and adaptive behavior.

Experiments have shown that stimulation of premature infants may have a positive effect on achievement, weight gain, and the nervous system's ability to organize a sleep pattern. Kathryn Barnard, of the University of Washington in Seattle, reported at a meeting of the American Academy of Child Psychiatry how the stimulation of seven premature infants by rocking and by allowing them to hear heartbeat sounds resulted in their making greater gains than a control group of eight other premature babies.

We should note here that while stimulation provided by way of movement, touch, and sight is extremely important, infants vary in their need for and response to it. Dr. Anneliese Korner, of the Stanford University School of Medicine, noted that infants ". . . will vary markedly from each other in how much they initiate interaction with their mothers and as a consequence, how much caretaking they will elicit." She states that babies vary both in irritability and in how easily they are soothed and how long they remained comforted. In her studies, she found that the experience of being picked up and moved did more than simple body contact in soothing a baby and causing him to be more alert. Of course, most activities with a newborn infant will involve both touch and movement. Dr. Korner feels that, at least in the earliest days of a child's life, the movement stimulation may be more important than touch and body contact alone. Normal infants will vary in how cuddly they are. Some babies may be born with special sensitivities. For example, an occasional infant will experience touch as painful. If this can be recognized early, steps may be taken so that difficulties do not result. Dr. Reginald Lourie gives an example of a mother whose baby's hypersensitivity was responsible for his irritability and turning away from her. On hearing this, the mother said, "Let me put him on a pillow and hold the pillow when I feed him if it's important for him to have closeness. That doesn't make him uncomfortable."

Korner writes that ". . . very sensitive babies tend to become overwhelmed with overstimulation unless a mothering person acts as a shield and tension-reducing agent." In contrast, there may be babies who have high sensory thresholds and may require significantly more stimulation for optimal development.

All of this is important in a full consideration of the early care of infants. It reiterates the uniqueness of each situation and each infant-parent relationship. Again it shows the complexities involved in the raising of children and the difficulties inherent in trying to advise parents as to the best way to fulfill their roles. We know that stimulation is important, but we also know that, in infants, there are great individual differences involved. In addition to this, each parent brings his or her own background and attitude into the picture. Parenthood is a difficult art, and the foregoing indicates some of the problems and challenges involved.

Dr. Korner expresses the problem this way:

Certain child care practices and certain forms of early stimulation are considered universally beneficial regardless of a given child's needs. We are thus forever looking for THE method to raise children, to educate, to cure. One aspect of this trend is to see the mother and the care and stimulation she provides as almost solely responsible for the normality and deviation of her child's development. While this stance feeds into the illusion that with the "correct methods" and the "right attitudes" we are in control of our children's destiny, it also produces a lot of guilt. This, in turn, undercuts parental effectiveness in dealing flexibly with each child's strengths and vulnerabilities. . . . In working with parents it is important that we stress not only their crucial influence on their children's development, but also that we free them to see, to hear, to tune in, and to trust their own intuition in dealing differentially with what their children present as *separate* individuals.

There was a time, not terribly long ago, when the main emphasis concerning the infant's attachment to its mother was on the feeding process. It was believed that the satisfaction of the infant's hunger established the tie to the mother. When I started my pediatric training twenty-five years ago, we were given the equation, "food = mother, mother = love, therefore, food = love." No doubt, the satisfaction of hunger is still an important factor in the relationship between mother and infant, but it is not simply the nutritional aspect that comes into play. A feeding baby is cradled in his mother's arms and is receiving the benefit of touch. He is moved about by his mother and receives the benefit of motion. He is looked at by his mother and he looks at her, thereby engaging in visual activity. And presumably, the mother will talk to him, providing auditory stimulation.

The process of feeding an infant, then, is one in which the varied needs for stimulation can be met. When we begin to think about feeding infants, we come to the question of how is this best accomplished. Dr. Niles Newton, Professor of Psychology at Northwestern University School of Medicine, writes that in preliterate, preindustrial societies and in some present primitive societies, mothers practiced what can be called "unrestricted breast feeding." The infant usually slept in the mother's room or mother's bed and there were no rules to restrict sucking. In the early weeks of life, the infant might receive ten or more feedings per day and by the latter half of the first year this would gradually decrease to five or six per day. The infant was helped to the breast whenever he cried or fussed. Other foods were added only when the infant could swallow solids without gagging or when the presence of teeth showed that the child was ready to chew.

The feeding process, therefore, contributed much sensory stimulation and satisfaction to the infant, and the mother benefited both from caring for the infant and the physiological changes within her that resulted from the process of nursing. Breast milk continued to be a major source of nourishment beyond infancy into early childhood. With this type of breast-feeding, weaning came late, and there is probably a great deal of similarity between this and the nursing behavior described by Jane Goodall in her chimpanzee studies.

In our contemporary society, there has been a movement away from breast-feeding—at least from the free access to feeding and sucking which existed with unrestricted breast-feeding. When it is practiced at all, it is most often what has been described as "token breast-feeding."

Most girls today have been reared in families in which their mothers did not breast-feed. Even when a woman had a great desire to breast-feed, she often became discouraged because of the attitudes of her doctor, nurses, family, and friends. At one time, because of the dangers of infection and the possibility of poor nutrition, bottle-feeding was a second-best choice. However, with the advent of formulas of various types, improvements in bottles, and other aids, bottle-feeding has become simplified. One can find vigorous supporters on either side of the controversy as to whether breast- or bottle-feeding is the best. My personal opinion is that there are great advantages to breast-feeding—especially when a mother is particularly desirous of nursing her baby.

From the point of emotional development and from the aforementioned need for sensory stimulation, I feel that the mother and child will both benefit. The mother who honestly wants to breast-feed would find it difficult not to offer the infant a great deal of comfort and stimulation at the same time. This is not to say that a mother who bottle-feeds her baby cannot do the same thing, but she should try to reproduce a situation which would normally occur during breast-feeding. She should cradle the child in her arms, hold him close to her, and try to give him the accompanying benefits of touch, movement, sight, and sound.

There are mothers who may have a deeply ingrained antipathy to the idea of breast-feeding, and it would be a mistake for them to attempt. Other mothers are undecided on the question of breast-feeding. They should seek advice and encouragement. The setup in many hospitals and the attitudes of many health-care workers may sometimes tend to discourage them.

About seventeen years ago, a small group of women organized the La Leche League.* Its purpose was to supply information and encouragement to mothers who wanted to breast-feed. The organization has grown to a thousand groups

* La Leche League International, 9616 Minneapolis Avenue, Franklin Park, Illinois 60131.

located in forty-nine states and fourteen foreign countries. A mother who wonders whether or not she can or wishes to breast feed can obtain information from this pro-breast-feeding group.

The studies of early infancy highlight the importance of stimulation for the healthy development of the human infant. He needs to experience closeness to another human being and to receive the benefits of motion, touch, sight, and sound. In some instances, special temperamental and constitutional factors must be taken into consideration. The first eighteen months of a child's life are of utmost importance to the foundation of his future personality development.

Those of us who choose to be parents are, therefore, presented with an opportunity and a challenge. We must get to know our offspring during early infancy and try to provide them with what they need—and what they need is much more than mere food and shelter.

Chapter V

Separation Anxiety

Life, by its very nature, is full of situations where we must be separated from those to whom we feel close. This creates a feeling of discomfort—a sensation which is termed "separation anxiety."

Both ends of life—birth and death—involve separation. During pregnancy, the fetus is biologically part of the mother. At birth, it must make the short but difficult journey into our world and an independent physical existence. While still totally dependent for its care, it is now a separate human being. At the other end of life, we face the permanent separation of death. Feelings of separation are experienced by the dying person and by the surviving relatives and friends.

Between the poles of birth and death are many situations which may produce, to greater or lesser degrees, separation anxiety. A child's first day at school is generally such a situation. Or, when a young adult leaves home to attend college in another city. A marriage represents a kind of separation from family and may result in anxiety for the individuals beginning a new family unit.

Separation anxieties often are at the heart of unresolved problems. An example comes to mind from the time immediately following World War II when I was one of many physicians sent overseas to serve in the Army of Occupation. A young medical officer I knew was assigned to a hospital in a Far Eastern country. As far as comfortable surroundings and the possibility for interesting work were concerned, his setup was enviable compared to what most of us encountered in our own units. But before long, we heard that this competent young doctor was extremely depressed and often remained in his room crying. Eventually, he was sent back to the United States because he was unable to function in the hospital. Of course, I do not know exactly what this man's problems were, but I certainly do not believe that he was malingering in order to return home. Rather, I have always felt that he had a deep-seated difficulty with separation and that the emotional implications of being so far away from his home, friends, and family may have been too much for him to deal with.

I know several adults of substantial means who will not travel abroad because, for reasons they cannot explain, it makes them uncomfortable. Here again, I suspect that, in many of these cases, there are remnants of poorly handled separation anxiety which contributes to their discomfort.

How each individual deals with various episodes of separation may depend largely on how the initial experiences with separation anxiety were handled in our infancy and childhood. Earlier, we examined the importance of the infant becoming attached to at least one significant adult in his environment—usually the mother. At birth, the baby is relatively "unrelated" to this adult but, as his perceptions and awareness develop, he begins to conceive of himself as a dependent part of another human being. This normally occurs by three to five months. By the eighth or ninth month, the infant has the physical ability to crawl away from his mother, the person to whom he has become attached. It is at this age that we begin to see evidence of separation anxiety. The child has the means to move away and at the same time begins to fear the state of being away from the person who represents security to him. Here, too, we begin to observe the interplay between the need to be dependent and the drive to become independent.

At this stage of development, the infant also begins to be afraid of strangers. Often grandparents who have not been seeing the baby on a regular basis are upset to find that the grandchild, who only months before was friendly and easily held, now cries if they attempt to pick him up. They must understand that what is happening is a normal stage of separation anxiety, and they must give the infant time to become accustomed to their friendly presence.

Infants taken to the pediatrician during this stage may cry as soon as they are examined. The physician will probably have a much easier time if he talks to the mother first, before examining the child. This allows the child time to become accustomed to him and the situation. When the examination does take place, it will be less traumatic for all concerned. Babies experiencing this fear of strangers often cry if someone new simply stares at them.

During this period, an infant may cry if his mother leaves his sight, as though she would be gone forever. Some young mothers are at a loss as to what to do about the crying. One young woman, going to her pediatrician for a routine eight-month checkup, expressed the problem this way: "I don't know what I should do," she said. "All of a sudden, my son has begun to cry each time I leave him, even if I am just going into another room. My mother and mother-in-law tell me I will spoil him if I pick him up each time he cries, but this is what I feel I should do. Still, I am not sure I am doing the right thing.''

The pediatrician explained that the baby was beginning to be concerned about separation from her, and that if this stage were handled well, it might soon be over, at least in so acute a form. He suggested that for the time being she try not to leave him for prolonged periods. He also recommended that when she moved from one room to another she place the baby where he could still see her, so that he would come to understand that when she walked through a door she had not disappeared. He assured her that her intuitive desire to comfort the baby whenever she felt it necessary was more sound than her mother's and mother-in-law's fears that she would spoil the child. When she came in several months later, the mother reported that the child was no longer exhibiting the same kind of apprehension when she left his sight. Now it is impossible to know for sure what would have occurred had this mother handled the situation differently, but one could speculate that the child would have had more rather than less anxiety when inevitable periods of separation took place in the future.

Separation anxiety is a normal development during the third quarter of the first year. Understanding this can be a great help in handling the problem. At this stage, it is important for the baby to learn that his mother will usually be available. Prior to the fifth or sixth month, the infant may not be as affected by the absence of his primary caretaker, but from six months to three years, a child is likely to be more sensitive to separation. When an infant begins to show a fear of strangers and cries when his mother is out of sight, it is important for his parents to insure that there are no long periods of separation.

Of course, there will always be separations which we cannot prevent. The mother who goes to the hospital for the delivery of another baby will necessarily be separated from her other children during that time. Any illness requiring hospitalization will create separations of varying length.

There have been a number of studies attempting to determine the effects of separation on infants and children. A great deal of theorizing has been done on the basis of data collected on infants and children in institutions such as hospitals or foundling homes. Some twenty-two years ago, James Robertson of the Tavistock Clinic in London, described the effect of separation from their parents on children who had to be hospitalized. He described three stages in the child's reaction: protest, despair, and denial (which was later termed "detachment"). Similar types of behavior have been observed in monkeys deprived of their mothers.

More recently, Robertson and his wife, Joyce, observed four children in separate families who were not hospitalized, but who were separated from their mothers because of the impending arrival of a second child. The children involved were between one and a half to two and a half years—the usual age range for separation studies. They were all children who lived with both parents and who had not previously been separated from their mothers for longer than an occasional few hours, during which time they had been left in the care of a familiar person. The Robertsons served as the foster parents during each mother's confinement. During the month before separation, the children were introduced to the foster home and the foster family. On coming to the Robertsons' home, each child brought his own bed, blankets, toys, stuffed animals, and a photograph of his or her mother. Fathers were allowed to visit as often as they wished. At the end of the separation period, the child joined his mother in the presence of the foster mother and, in the following weeks, the foster mother visited the child's home several times.

Reporting on their experience with these children, the Robertsons say:

> By the time the children might have been expected to show despair [according to earlier studies], that is on the second, third, or fourth day, there was some sadness, a lowered frustration tolerance, and some aggression. But this did not have the quality of despair. By that point each child had developed a relationship to the foster mother sufficient to sustain him and had begun to cling to her. The relationship to the foster mother then held these children in a state of manageable anxiety. They used her increasingly and with growing intimacy. Although under considerable strain throughout, all four children cared for in our supportive foster situation functioned and related well, learned new skills and new words, and at reunion greeted their mothers warmly. The separation had not been traumatic. The children had not been overwhelmed.

A colleague of the Robertsons, Katrin Stroh, made observations on nine children who remained in their own homes while their mothers were having second babies. She, too, noted no immediate distress. After two to four days, the youngsters did become more irritable and would cling to their substitute caretakers; however, they all continued to eat as before and learned new words and skills. Their reunion with their mothers was smooth and pleasant.

The Robertsons' report on a seventeen-month-old child cared for in a residential nursery during his mother's absence contrasts sharply with the two studies just described. This child's parents, in consultation with their family physician, had chosen the residential nursery care, and the boy was admitted to a room with about five other children of the same age. Most of the children in the institution had been there from birth. The nurses were not assigned to individual youngsters and the personnel changed frequently because of times off and other duties. Therefore, this boy did not receive responsive substitute mothering and was exposed to the many stresses of an institutional environment. The child deteriorated in all areas while separated, and when reunited with his mother he rejected her with "struggles and desperate crying." The Robertsons felt that the difference between the reactions of their foster children and this little boy was a qualitative one and not merely one of degree. While the children they cared for came through the experience fairly well, the Robertsons conclude that it "does not mean that the hazards attached to early separation can be eliminated entirely. At that early and vulnerable phase of development even the best of substitute care is not a certain prescription for neutralizing the risks. . . . The complexities which commonly affect substitute care are such to reinforce the view that separation is dangerous and should, whenever possible, be avoided."

Recently I saw a ten-and-a-half-year-old boy for psychiatric consultation because he exhibited unusual outbursts of anger, especially toward his mother. This youngster had been adopted at eight months of age. His history showed that he had been in the care of apparently good foster parents until the time of his adoption. His adoptive parents were well-meaning, conscientious people who wanted him very much, who loved him, and who were extremely concerned about his welfare. He had been well treated, but still exhibited unreasonable outbursts of anger. When his mother asked him why he became so angry he would say, "I was born that way."

When we discussed his adoption procedure, the parents told me that the eight-month-old infant cried for twenty-four hours after they brought him home. After this, he seemed to regress in his development—or at least ceased to progress. He did not sit up until he was ten months old, and his adoptive parents were concerned. His mother recalls vividly that, after ten months, he did not seem to have the least bit of interest in food or the feeding process. Yet just before they took him to their home he had been described as a "fat, happy baby."

After some time, this baby did begin to progress again in his physical growth and development. I could see from the history that at eight months he had gone through the stages of protest and despair which James Robertson described in the hospitalized child. Fortunately, because of the care and attention he received from his adoptive parents, he did not go on to the stage of detachment. However, I feel that his problem with anger may well have been connected to the separation and abandonment which he experienced in the sudden shift from foster parents to adopting parents at eight months, an age where separation anxiety is high.

His father expressed it this way, "It was wrong for us to have to take him suddenly like that. We should have had a chance to go visit on several occasions and become accustomed to each other." There is, no doubt, much truth in this. In cases where adoption of infants occurs past the first month or two of life, we should be particularly concerned with the effects of separation from foster parents or caretakers, especially if the infant has had good, loving care. Efforts should be made to prevent or mitigate the type of situation that this youngster experienced.

I think it is important for us to pay attention to the findings of people who are studying the effects of separation under normal circumstances. These findings indicate that when separation is necessary, we should try to leave the child in as familiar surroundings as possible and in the care of someone with whom he is familiar. Parents should also keep in mind that the young child will probably have some feeling of anger toward the parent for having ''left'' him for the particular period of time, and the parent may have some fence-mending to do when he or she returns home.

It should be mentioned here that one of the essential reasons for a father to be more involved in the daily care of his child is so that the youngster can develop a feeling of attachment to him. This bond to the father can be an ameliorating factor if the mother must be separated from the child. When parents know beforehand that there will have to be a separation from both of them, however, every effort should be made to provide a familiar substitute in familiar surroundings.

As with other aspects of child-raising, I feel that the problem of separation raises conflicts between what parents want to do and what may be best for them, and what may be best for the child. Take, for example, the matter of vacations. Often, one hears parents say that they ''must get away from the children for a few weeks.'' In some instances, where parents have an extremely hyperactive child, it would be difficult to disagree. Certainly, with all children, it is important for parents to spend periodic evenings and other times without their children (with the children being cared for by a competent baby-sitter whom they know). However, when we are considering children below the age of four or five years, we should be very aware of the possible bad effects which might result from separations of over a day or two. If I were considering only the welfare of children, I would suggest to parents that they not take vacations away from the children that extend past two days until their children are past five years of age. In any event, as I mentioned in a preceding chapter, they absolutely must make every effort to provide caretakers who are competent and trustworthy and with whom the children are acquainted.

I realize that whatever the evidence regarding the effects of separation, there will still be many people who feel it is more important to "get away" than to remain home or take their children with them on vacation. These parents should be prepared for the possibility that the young child will be angry with them or reject them upon their return. Or he might cling to them and not want to let them out of his sight. In some instances, a youngster may act as if he does not want even to look at his mother or acknowledge that she still exists. Such a child is reacting to the effects of separation and will need reassurance that the parent is present and will not soon be leaving again.

One of the most common problem periods regarding separation is when the child first goes off to school. The youngster's reaction may depend on a variety of factors. He simply may be less adaptable than others to new situations or he may bring with him unresolved anxiety about separation—and the experience of the first days in school without his parents is therefore very frightening. Some parents carry within themselves old scars of separations that occurred in their own childhood—through death, divorce, or abandonment. These parents may find it difficult to give the child the type of support which would enable him to cope with and overcome the anxious feelings connected with separation.

A four-year-old girl recently started nursery school. She seemingly enjoyed it, but did not want to go in the car pool unless her mother went with her. The mother wondered whether or not to keep the child in the nursery school since she had these problems about separation. She decided to go along with the child for awhile and at the same time encourage the feeling that the girl was growing up and could enjoy school by herself without her mother's presence. The child gradually became accustomed to being away from her mother during the short nursery-school day. She now goes, enjoys it, and has overcome a good bit of her fear of separation from her mother.

In older children, we occasionally see a condition which has been termed "school phobia." This refusal to go to school may start out with the child complaining of physical symptoms such as headaches or abdominal pains. Once the child remains home for any length of time, it sometimes becomes extremely difficult to get him back to school. It is possible that there is a realistic problem in school—such as learning disability, a class bully, or an unreasonable teacher. But often, it is none of these factors. Rather, it is an underlying anxiety about separation from home and parents. In many instances, the children involved have parents with separation anxiety problems of their own. If a child refuses to go to school and cannot be reasonably made to do so, the parents should seek some professional help in determining what the underlying problems might be.

The fact remains that separation anxiety is a sensation which we all have to deal with at times throughout our lives. Bearing this in mind, we should be particularly cognizant of how our presence—or absence—can affect our children's feelings of security. When parents work and leave their children in the care of others, the youngsters still see their parents every day. This experience of partial separation presents some disadvantages, but does not seem to have quite the adverse effects of longer separations, such as those involving vacations or hospitalization.

I repeat that, particularly from birth to four or five years, the cause of healthy emotional development in children will be best served by having their parents interested in them and available to them. When separations become necessary, parents should make every effort to provide familiar substitutes in familiar surroundings. The adequate resolution of a child's separation anxieties at the time they occur can go a long way toward insuring his ability to function successfully and happily throughout his entire life.

Chapter VI

The Development of Independence

There does come a time, of course, when the child must be gradually weaned from total dependence and taught to be self-reliant. We often hear people say, "That mother ought to cut the cord." Of course, the expression refers to the figurative umbilical cord rather than the physical severing of a newborn's no-longer-useful lifeline to his mother.

It is true that many individuals make what appears to be unsatisfactory progress toward independence. For example, the adult who lives at home with his parents and never manages to establish an adult relationship makes us wonder about the lack of mature resolution of his ties to his parents.

In more affluent families, I often detect a subtle brand of child dependence which is fostered by parents. In these families, young people are given homes, furniture, automobiles, and other material objects at the beginning of their married lives. What bothers me here is when the older generation refers to their children's possessions as "our house" or "the new car we're buying." They help out financially, but there are strings attached which keep the children in a dependent

73

position. It is as if the parents are saying by their actions, "While we have the ability to give you financial aid, we have not provided you with an adequate independent personality which would enable you to use these gifts wisely." When a young man or woman asks a parent for aid or advice, the interchange can be beneficial to both parties. However, in the long run, imposed and ongoing control helps neither. To me, this indicates that the parents have failed to permit their youngsters to grow into independent adults.

As with any concept as abstract as this, we could get into a great deal of discussion as to what constitutes independence. There is no absolute or perfect example of this or any other characteristic. We do know, however, that the newborn infant is completely dependent on his caretakers for survival. We can learn about independence by tracing his development from this point of helplessness through the various stages to the point where he can take care of himself and, hopefully, when the time arrives, others as well. Many people I've talked with over the years conceive of an independent person as one who never needs anyone else and is therefore totally self-sufficient. And certain people act as if independence means having absolutely nothing to do with one's parents. I can't help but wonder about the emotional make-up of either children or parents who feel this way.

My own concept of the independent adult is the person who has reached the point where he or she can be interdependent. By this, I mean a person who can rely on others and have others rely on him, but who can also function adequately by himself. A husband and wife who feel they can depend on each other when the need arises are a good example of individuals who have reached such a point in their development. Such a relationship is quite different from one in which a wife is completely dependent on her husband for her emotional well-being, or vice versa. When a child is added to a family, the independent adult will not be threatened by a rival for the spouse's attention. Rather, the parents should be able, individually and together, to minister to the needs of this new member of their family.

The question is, how does one make the journey from total dependency, through states of increasing independence, to the realm of interdependency? There are those who feel this is best accomplished by forcing a large degree of "independence" on a child early in life. Twenty-five years ago, for example, an article appeared in a national weekly newsmagazine describing a doctor who was beginning to feed newborn infants solid food in the second and third days of life. His rationale was that this practice would hasten the infant's development of independence. From the standpoint of nutrition and physiology, this too-early introduction of solid food simply does not make sense. Solid food is nutritionally unnecessary at so early an age, and the infant's nervous system and digestive apparatus are not ready for it. The very act of swallowing the food may be unpleasant for the baby. So instead of experiencing the feeding process as a pleasant proposition during which his hunger is satisfied, the infant who has solid food forced into him before he is ready may develop unpleasant associations.

But aside from these physical considerations, let us get back to the concept of early solid feeding fostering independence in children. Even if such a concept were sound (and I do not believe it is), we would have to wonder whether the attempt to create independence so early is necessarily a good thing. My belief is that independence should not be forced upon children. It should proceed and evolve out of the normal course of their development. By and large, the "average" child should achieve independence as a result of his progression through the various stages of infancy, child-hood, and adolescence.

Too often in adult life (and particularly in my profession), we are confronted with problems in those who have not had their dependency needs met. The infant and child has a very real need to be cared for; yet, there sometimes are instances where these requirements are not met. This may occur out of ignorance—when the parents simply do not understand or re-alize how important it is. Or, the parents may have emotional problems that make them unaware of their child's needs or unavailable to deal with them. Illness, death of a parent, so-cioeconomic deprivation, or any number of other factors may stand in the way of a child having his dependency taken care of. And then there are those parents who say that what they want to do takes precedence over the needs of their children and the youngsters will have to fit in as best they can. It is the latter group of parents I wish had made the decision not to have children.

It is often true that parents with such an attitude were themselves the victims of unmet dependency needs in infancy and childhood. Whatever the cause, we can see evidence of the void some people seem to have in relationship to depen-dency, and we can see some of the problems created by their efforts to fill this void. I came across an example of this dur-ing my psychiatric training when I was a resident in a general hospital. One of my functions was to conduct consultations with patients when their physicians felt emotional problems were interfering with the prescribed medical treatments. One of the patients was a young adult with moderately severe diabetes. It was important to his health that he follow the prescribed diet and that he take his medication regularly. He was an intelligent young man, but for some reason, he con-tinued to be irresponsible about his diet and medication.

Time after time, he would end up in the hospital with his diabetes completely out of control. At times, he was practically comatose. His attending physician could not understand why this seemingly competent young man would not, or could not, take care of himself. In meeting and talking with this patient, it appeared to me that he had a great reservoir of unfilled dependency needs. While he realized that he had a serious illness and that he should take care of himself, the need to be taken care of by others was so great that he neglected his treatment so that he would have to go back to the hospital, where he would be taken care of. He may not have made the decision consciously, but it certainly appeared to be a case of his reason not being able to overcome his deep-seated emotional need. In his own mind, when he was ill, it was permissible to allow himself to be cared for.

Most physicians recognize that many of the symptoms and psychosomatic illnesses they see can be tied to underlying dependency needs. Children often use illness, real or feigned, to get their parents' time and attention when they feel they cannot get it any other way.

In my view, it is crucial to the development of independence for the infant and child to have his fill of dependence. It is like the story of the tailor who claimed that if he had to err in making a pair of pants, he would always want to err on the side of making them too long. He could always fix them by shortening each leg, but if he made them too short, his work would be worthless and he would have to begin again. This type of reasoning also applies to children, although it is clear that in this case, a severe mistake cannot be alleviated by beginning again. But what I mean by the above example is that it would be better to err on the side of giving a child too much attention (if there is such a thing) than too little.

It can, of course, be bad to "smother" a child, but this is

something quite different from giving him attention. This usually means that the youngster has been overprotected and has not been permitted to learn to take care of himself. In some cases, mothers who may not have wanted a child react to their feelings of rejection by completely submerging them and consciously or unconsciously bending over backward in the opposite direction. They might hover over the child to a degree that is stultifying to his growth and development. This type of parental behavior can be placed at one extreme of the spectrum. At the other end is the parent who rejects and neglects the child. And as with all aspects of human behavior, one can find almost infinite gradations between these extremes. It is much easier to determine what is outright rejection and neglect, however, than it is to determine when attention is becoming a pathological form of overprotection. While neglect is certainly the worst of the evils, the total smothering of a child will not fulfill a child's dependency needs either.

The important thing to remember here is that a child should not be forced into independence. We see, in many of our poverty areas, children who are forced to grow up before their time. They must take on unreasonable obligations in caring for themselves and their siblings or helping to earn money for the family's support years before such a job would be beneficial in teaching "responsibility." The fact that they must assume this burden does not necessarily promote an adequate type of independence when they are older. In fact, this premature and forced independence may prevent them from making proper use of their childhood in terms of formal education or preparation for comfortable adulthood and parenthood. Each of us probably knows of individuals who had such responsibility in childhood and who turned out to be fine, happy human beings. But those, I am afraid, are simply outstanding people who are exceptions to the rule.

Generally speaking, I believe it is better for a child to be more, rather than less dependent *if the parents are able to let go when he becomes an adolescent and young adult.* The child needs to know that when problems come up there is someone who will help him to solve them. This does not mean that we should do everything for him. There is a vast difference between the parent who will do a child's homework for him so that he will always have it correct and the parent who lets the child know of his availability if there is something he does not understand. Over the years, I have observed that some of the best examples of independent individuals are those adults who were given every opportunity as children to be dependent on their parents.

The dependency needs of different individuals will also vary according to the circumstances. The mildly or seriously handicapped child will usually have a need to be more dependent than other children. Differences in temperament of infants can affect the degree of dependency they will exhibit. What is important is that parents be aware of the dependency need and try to meet it.

The material discussed in the preceding chapters relates directly to the question of meeting a child's needs. The beginnings of the feelings of trust and reliability that the child requires occur in infancy. The establishment of the bonds between the infant and his mother and father will affect the child's security for a long time to come. These same bonds may also affect the parents' ability to meet their obligations in relationship to their offspring. If one fulfills the early demands for attention in a satisfactory manner, those demands will usually decrease steadily as the child becomes older and moves through each stage of development. But it is extremely important that the child have a feeling of trust in, and reliance on, adults devoted to him and to his welfare.

When I speak of meeting a child's needs, I am by no means implying that a parent should indulge the child's every whim. Anyone who attempts such a course will soon recognize its futility. An excessively overprotective or overindulgent parent could retard the child's development. Children must learn to tolerate frustration. Hopefully, they will experience it in small doses rather than be overwhelmed by it. Just as in allergic conditions a patient is given minute doses of the material he is allergic to in order to develop resistance and immunity, so must the infant and young child be exposed to small and tolerable degrees of frustration to learn to deal successfully with it. Here, as in other areas of child health and development, we must keep in mind the variations in an individual's ability to tolerate frustration. It is necessary for parents to get to know and understand the make-up of their particular child. Feelings of frustration in an infant are unavoidable. Even when a mother breast-feeds a baby and there is no delay due to preparation or heating of a bottle, there will still be a time lapse between the moment when the baby's hunger makes him uncomfortable and the moment when his mother is able to give him the breast. It is important for the child to learn to tolerate frustration, but he must also know that there is someone there to take care of him and help him.

The most important factor is the presence of the parent or a competent caring substitute. The child must know that there is someone he can go to at any time. The presence of caring adults is also necessary for the physical well-being of children. The greatest cause of death among children is accidents. According to the National Safety Council, approximately 15,000 young people between the ages of one and fourteen lose their lives because of accidents each year. Over seventeen million more are injured. Shockingly, it is estimated that nine out of every ten of the most serious accidents could have been prevented with proper care and supervision. Admittedly, not all accidents can be prevented; yet, in many cases, the presence of a thoughtful, aware parent or parent substitute can insure the child's safety. It is obvious that a child should be able to depend on his parents for his safety.

It is tempting to try to give parents exact prescriptions for when this or that degree of independence should be encouraged. However, one of the difficulties is that each child is different in make-up and each set of parents will need to determine what is best for their own children. I am more comfortable in assuring parents that the child who is permitted to be dependent when he needs to be will be more apt to be independent when he is grown. During the first two years particularly, he should have the security of knowing he will be taken care of. As he grows, his age and stage of development should be taken into account in determining what should be expected of him by way of independence. Most children have a built-in drive to be "normal." It is amazing to see the extent to which children overcome adverse circumstances in their environment in order to proceed with their development. A child will let us know, if we are tuned in, when he is ready for more independence. We should also be cognizant that maturity does not always follow a steady forward progression. Two steps ahead in development may be followed by a step backward. However, the child will usually resume his forward progress unless some roadblock, such as an illness or emotional problem, prevents it.

At certain points, a child will show that he is reaching a

milestone in the continuing balance between dependence and independence. When a child begins to be negativistic or "difficult," it often indicates he is discovering a will of his own and he wants to exercise it. This normally begins at about fifteen months and continues for some time. The child says "no" even to things he might want. And while he is active and exploring and beginning to move away from his caretaker, he still wants that person to be nearby.

What matters, then, is for each of us to be prepared to allow a child to be dependent on us when he needs to be. We should be aware of whatever evidence he presents to us of his readiness for more independence in his actions. Generally, it is not necessary that we push him into independent action in order to make him independent when he grows up. We should be prepared to give him the time and attention he needs. I do not believe we will spoil children by paying attention to them.

But if a child feels he can rely on the significant adults about him, he will have the best chance of feeling good and worthwhile and eventually be able to function as an interdependent adult human being. As I said earlier, it is not necessary that we "do" everything for a child. The key word is "support."

Chapter VII

The Family

All around us these days, we hear comments about the obsolescence of the family. From professionals in the human behavior and related fields and the public at large comes a hue and cry—the family is outmoded and has outlived its usefulness. A myriad of problems—separation and divorce, juvenile delinquency, drug abuse, mistreatment of children, and dissatisfaction of women—are cited as evidence that the family as the primary base for raising children just is not working.

Various alternatives are put forth as being better than the individual unit of a mother, father, and one or more children. Some recommend communes. Others propose turning over the major responsibility of child care to daily caretakers who could ameliorate what they consider the harmful effects of close family living. In my opinion, the family has not outlived its function or its usefulness, and we would be well advised to try to strengthen it rather than throw up our hands and discard it. Over the years, it has been my impression that most of the children who fare well in life are those who have been beneficiaries of a good family life, where both mother and father considered their roles a most important part of their daily existence.

While many critics are suggesting that children do not need a family life, I would suggest that they need a *better* type of family life. There are many changes taking place, and a strong family is necessary to help a child adjust to them. The world, for example, is becoming much smaller. Foreign lands and cultures are increasingly accessible to the population through the technological advances of jet travel and through the impact of television. Our children are exposed at younger and younger ages to events which in previous generations could have been kept from them altogether. An entire generation of children witnessed firsthand the grief and tragedy attending President John Kennedy's assassination and funeral. An actual war, thousands of miles away in Vietnam, came into our homes in living color on the Six O'clock News. I do not want to give the impression from this that I feel television is a negative influence. Rather, I feel it has the potential for being a tremendously positive one and we have not paid sufficient attention to many of its implications. However, television is also a primary example of the increased stimuli that even the preschool child is subjected to. Parents should be aware of what their children are seeing and be prepared to discuss programs with them.

Drugs are another fact of our changing world—in some areas of our country, drug use has filtered down to the fifth and sixth grades. Increasingly, parents of teen-agers complain that they can do nothing to control their children. They worry about the dangers and influences their offspring will be exposed to in school and in the community.

I certainly agree that youngsters today are living in a world where they are exposed to situations which potentially can be very damaging. The long-term effects of the so-called sexual revolution are yet to be determined, but children are being faced with decisions which can have great impact on both their physical and emotional well-being. The Vietnam War, the Watergate incident, and all the questions of morality involved in those issues have had an unquestionable effect on many of our young people. Increased mobility of many families creates problems. The emphasis in advertising on the acquisition of material possessions causes pressure for parents and children.

In my view, children need to come into their adolescence better fortified to deal with the world they find themselves in—they need more, rather than less, from the family in order to cope with life as it is now. For example, there was a time when it required a certain type of adventuresomeness on the part of a young person to experiment with marijuana. Today, I am told by high school and college students that it often takes "guts" to attend a party and not partake when drugs are offered.

We need to provide our children with an environment which will aid them in coping. I would like to see each of our young people develop his sense of individuality and self-worth so that he feels he has some control over what is happening to him.

To me, the family is the vehicle for accomplishing much of this. Over and over, I have seen that in those situations where children have turned out well, even under certain trying and adverse circumstances, it was largely due to the support given within the framework of the family. The adolescent has a need to rebel, and this rebellion will manifest itself in various ways. The worst rebellion is sometimes by those children who have had few limitations of any kind placed on them during childhood.

In thinking of the family as the best available setting for raising children, I find myself returning to my statement that prospective parents should really consider whether they want children and are willing to devote the necessary time and energy to properly care for them. It is of no use to say that "the Family" is good for children if the particular family turns out to be a bad one.

One of the main requisites for a good family is a husband and wife who love and respect each other and who together are willing to assume the responsibilities of family life. In our culture, one of the primary obligations is the provision of food, shelter, and other necessities for the members of the family. But were we to be relieved of the necessity of providing food and shelter for our children, we would still face the responsibility of caring for their emotional and intellectual development. Children need to learn about how they should conduct their own lives and what their own values should be. As they get older, they will be exposed to the values of their peer groups, and of the community in general. They will be comparing their own standards with those of others. What they have learned within the confines of their family group becomes tremendously important, for it becomes the basis on which they can evaluate their own beliefs in relation to those around them.

I often feel we do ourselves a disservice by neglecting what may be considered old-fashioned concepts. We become enmeshed in trying to explain human behavior on the basis of esoteric theories. In the process, we forget that individuals learn how to behave by following examples, not theories. What I have especially in mind is one of the most important concepts which can and should be taught within the framework of the family—that of responsibility.

We should remember that from the moment a child is born

he is learning from those around him, especially his parents. One of the first things he learns is trust, providing he is lovingly nurtured and cared for. To tell a child repeatedly, "I love you" is useless if the youngster recognizes that the actions of his parents are not in keeping with these words. I cannot stress enough that what we do is much more important than what we merely say.

In order to "indoctrinate" the child with the feeling that he should be a responsible person, we need to show him by our actions that we fulfill our own responsibilities as parents. A short time ago, I was appalled to read in a national magazine that in a number of recent divorce cases neither parent wanted custody of the children. Now I have to ask myself, how can we expect children to develop an independent sense of responsibility if their parents indicate through their actions that they are unwilling to fulfill their own rightful obligations?

In my office, I frequently see children who complain that school is boring. Undoubtedly, much of the schooling is tedious. Learning facts and basic skills is not always the most entertaining business in the world, but rather than trying to understand the reason for the work, these children seem to be under the impression that everything must be fun. They have not learned that sometimes one should tolerate unappealing work that may lead to greater benefit later on. When I see children like this, I begin to wonder what sort of message they are getting from their parents' actions and how this is reflected in the everyday family situation.

Taking care of children is not always fun. It requires of parents a great deal of self-denial as part of the carrying-out of responsibility. And soon enough, our children recognize whether or not we are acting in a responsible manner toward them. They will notice if we fulfill our obligations or make the pursuit of pleasure our primary purpose. Only if we teach by word and deed that we are responsible people can we rightfully expect the proper degree of responsibility from them.

Responsibility is just one of the values a family can, and should, inculcate in children. We may all differ in our concepts of right and wrong, but most of us believe that it is our right and duty to pass our standards of morality along to our young. The family should be like a laboratory for children, where they can begin to learn about life and how to deal with their feelings and perceptions. They should learn about their rights and how they relate to the rights of others. They should learn that not everything in life can be entertaining or fun, and that one must learn to tolerate frustration. In this sense, the family becomes a society in microcosm for the child, a give-and-take situation in which everyone contributes to the well-being of everyone else and the society as a whole. The family can be a setting in which the members can "fight" with each other and for each other and experience a necessary feeling of "belonging."

Another area where the family can instill important values to a child is that of sex. Today's increased openness in discussing sex is, on the whole, a salutary development. However, it is disturbing at times to see the lack of responsibility many young people demonstrate in the management of their sexual impulses, and it is also upsetting to me that too often sex becomes increasingly separated from intimacy.

It is within the confines of the family that a child can develop a great deal of his attitude about sex. He will learn by having his questions answered honestly and appropriately in keeping with his age. But the youngster learns also by what he sees of how his parents treat each other. He will see if his parents are affectionate and demonstrative with each other, and whether or not they treat each other with respect and consideration. From infancy, the child can experience the comfort and pleasure that comes from tactile stimulation. As he grows older, it becomes important for parents to continue to be demonstrative to the youngster, but to exercise care in helping the child by not overstimulating him. If husband and wife have a good relationship, can accept and enjoy their own sexuality, and are committed to the task of caring for their youngsters, the children will more than likely grow up with a healthy attitude toward sex.

It is true that some parents are incapacitated to a certain extent by their own emotional problems. But rather than to say as a result that the family has outlived its usefulness, we should better try to help these individuals. I do not believe that because there are more divorces, more drug abuse, and more battered children that the family has outlived its usefulness. Too often, we look at what is negative rather than at what is positive. From my own observations, I know that there are still many young people who have received the benefits that can be derived from a good family life. They have a strong sense of right and wrong and a solid concept of who they are, what they want to do, where they are going, and how they feel they ought to treat people. These are attitudes which they have derived mainly from the care, interest, and, in general, the "education" received within the framework of their immediate family. It is the foundation on which the structure of their personality has been built. This does not imply that they will be exactly like their parents. As individuals, they will modify and filter what they see through their own experience.

We are living in an era when our children have reason to question the morals and ethics of their elders. Our highest elected officials have been shown to be dishonest. There is more of a need than ever before to teach our offspring that there is a difference between right and wrong, rather than that anything you do is all right if you do not get caught. A better quality of family life is necessary at present when, in too many instances, parents are absenting themselves from their children. Adults do have a need for outside activities and interest, but there should be a balancing of this with the needs of a family.

I believe that parents who are interested in their children and who are willing to carry out the obligations of parenthood within the family are the best transmitters of the proper type of values. Perhaps, someday, we may find there is a better setting for raising children than within the individual family, but for the present, I do not believe anyone has found it.

In a book entitled *Are Parents Bad for Children?* the author, Graham B. Blaine, Jr., M.D., stated that while he did not believe we should abandon the family concept at this point, the care of children should be undertaken by community schools beginning at the age of three months. Under the plan, the children would be cared for from 8 a.m. to 6 p.m., six days a week, eleven months a year.

My own feeling is that our schools certainly should be improved. Facilities of the best possible sort should be provided for disadvantaged children but, in general, the primary responsibility for the care of children should continue to rest with their parents. I do not think there is any caretaker who will have the interest in a child that a devoted parent will. We ''experts'' would do better to try to impart to parents what we have discovered about human growth and development, so that they can function better in their current role.

There is much for children to learn in the realm of intellectual knowledge, in the matter of feelings and how to handle them, and in the area of value systems. And as far as I am concerned, the family is still the best place for basic training in these areas. Instead of scrapping what may be the best mechanism ever designed for the job, we should each evaluate how we can make it run more smoothly.

Chapter VIII

The Matter of Time

WHAT A KID WILL COST YOU—SCARY BEDTIME READING!

This quotation graced the cover of the March 1974 issue of *Esquire* magazine. Inside the periodical, the theme of which was "Do Americans Suddenly Hate Kids?" was a series of tables presented under the title, "The High Cost of Childhood." Beginning with conception and going through graduate school, the figures indicated that it would cost $203,026 to raise one good-to-superior educated male in a major city. The cost of raising a girl was slightly higher at $214,776. All of these were "direct costs." The parent so inclined could add life insurance costs of, say, $16,201, and another $101,430, representing the mother's loss of approximately fifteen years of employment income (figured at $6,762 per year). Most of us, from time to time, realize how much of a financial sacrifice we are making for our children, but seeing the figures laid out in black and white tends to boggle the mind.

When people contemplate the question of whether or not to have children, the financial cost of raising them is definitely a major consideration, and for some of us, a deciding factor. It would certainly not be a good idea to have children knowing that there would not be the economic wherewithal to supply them with adequate food, shelter, clothing, and educational or vocational opportunities.

But as important as the financial aspects of raising children can be, when I consider the requirements of parenthood and the needs of children, the matter of time becomes a much more important factor. Most adults are responsible enough to manage adequately the economics of money. But as far as I am concerned, we need to do a great deal more thinking about what might be called the "economics of time."

We all know, or have heard of, individuals who have suffered severe financial reverses after having accumulated great wealth. In many cases, they are able to apply the knowledge and talents which made them their fortunes to reaccumulate financial assets. Any of us who loses a lot of money has at least the possibility of working to acquire more. But as we all should know, this is not true of time. Once lost, time can never be regained. It is the most valuable of commodities and cannot be bought with any other.

I am convinced that most of us are extremely wasteful of time. The older we get, the more we may become aware of how quickly "time flies." Yet we continue to handle time carelessly. We hear people say, "I have to kill some time," or "I've got a couple of hours to waste." I am not suggesting that we fill every waking moment; that is impossible. I do believe, however, that we often pay more attention to money and its acquisition than we do to time. Parents give allowances to their children and frequently expect the youngsters to learn to budget for themselves. How often, however, through word or personal example, do we teach them to pay as much attention to the value of time?

Most of us can remember being back in elementary school and waiting impatiently to get to junior high and high school. Once there, we could not wait to get to college or to work. For some, college was just a necessary way station on the road to graduate schools or professional training of various kinds. We were always eager to move along to the next step. Meanwhile, the years inexorably went by with few of us having the capacity to enjoy the present. We need to look at all of the ramifications of the ways we handle time, but in this book, I am mainly concerned with the question of the time parents devote to their children. As I have mentioned in previous chapters, there is no doubt that there are built-in conflicts between the needs of children and the needs of parents. What we end up with are compromises between them. In most instances, the very years that children need to have their parents around them are the same years during which most parents (particularly fathers) are busily engaged in building up a business or profession. When the parent has "made it" and feels secure in his job, he might be willing to spend more time with his offspring. But he often finds that the infant has become a teen-ager and has gotten quite used to the father or mother not being around. The parent has lost his best chance of knowing his child and passing on to him a sense of his own values and perspectives on life. So many parents and children find that they really do not know each other.

I do not know how successful we can be in teaching our children to value time, but I have no doubt that we should make the attempt. As in most things relating to child-raising, they will learn as much, or more, by our example as by our words. The amount of time we are willing to spend with our children should be determined as nearly as possible before the decision to have children is made. Because, once they are here, the amount of time spent with them is often a crucial determinant in their development and later happiness in life.

Over my years of practicing psychotherapy with children, I have often tried to analyze what it was that actually enabled certain children to benefit from treatment. In some cases, of course, the answer has been obvious. These are instances in which a youngster harbors certain illogical or unreasonable ideas about relationships or feelings. Given an opportunity to discuss them candidly in a confidential setting, he may be relieved of unreasonable guilt or hostility, can give up his symptoms, and proceed with his development. There are other youngsters, however, who come to therapy sessions and say little about their feelings or fantasies. They do not object to coming but their verbal communication is minimal. Yet many of them improve markedly, and they, too, can proceed with their development. What is it that occurs during treatment with this latter group of young patients?

When I attempt to answer this question, I think back on my own experience as a parent. I have always tried to be aware that children need their parents around, and I have tried to see to it that I was involved with my children and was available to them. But I realized that while I could remember many instances of the whole family being together, I could recall only infrequent times when an individual child would have as much as a whole hour of my undivided attention. The child patient who comes to see me in my office gets 50 minutes of my undivided attention, and I think this fact largely explains why a noncommunicative child still benefits from therapy. The simple knowledge on a child's part that there is an adult interested in him who is willing to spend time with him, can go a long way toward having that child feel better about himself. And this is at least as true in the home as in the psychiatrist's office.

The child who benefits most from my attention during therapy often is lacking sufficient attention in his home setting. The main point I would like to get across to parents is how important it is for the parent to be with his child in order to see, to hear, to help, to explain, to share feelings, to comfort, to encourage attempts at tasks even if the child fails in his efforts.

There is another aspect to be considered. Imagine how the child of two busy parents must feel. As he becomes old enough to be aware, he may notice that his father is totally occupied by his profession during the day. When he comes home, he has a drink and reads the paper. After dinner, he may have office work to do or he may be involved in meetings or in community activities. On the weekends, there is golf, tennis, or some other form of recreation to relieve the accumulated pressures of the week. Mother, if she has a career, can be every bit as busy as Father. If she does not have a career, she may be involved in volunteer work. She may spend time with golf, tennis, or bridge. Shopping can take up several hours on any given day. At various times during the year, the parents may be away on trips, either for business or vacation.

This may all seem like a tremendously exaggerated picture. Let me assure you that, for many families, it is not. Even mothers who are home all day may be so preoccupied with household and other chores that they actually devote little time to being with their children in a meaningful way.

In any event, it does not take much imagination to see what the child of two very busy parents might be thinking and what he might be feeling about himself and his own worth. He could be saying to himself, "My mother and father are doing all these things that are so important to them. They don't spend much of their time with me. If I'm not important enough for them to spend time with, I must not be worth very much." It is not at all inconceivable that such a child would have low self-esteem, based on his observations that he is not of much value to those who are the most important people in his early life.

Some children find that the only way they can get their parents' time and attention is by being ill. Some will feign illness and others develop actual psychosomatic symptoms. It is extremely depressing to me to think of children needing to be sick in order to "get through" to their parents.

Repeatedly, I have heard people say, "It is the quality of time you spend with children that matters rather than the quantity." The notion is by now so widespread that it has a cliché quality to it. But in many cases, this statement has been used as a rationalization by people who just are not spending enough time with their children.

I would never quarrel with the concept that the quality of time we spend with children is of utmost importance. We all realize that a mother or father can be physically in the presence of a child for long periods of time and yet not really "be" with the child. A mother who is depressed and unhappy at being at home all day may be less available in terms of the child's emotional, social, and intellectual development than a working mother who, when she comes home, actually does devote her time and interest to her child.

However, I feel that the quantity of time a parent spends with a child is also highly significant. A parent who sits the child down and says, "Tell me what's on your mind" or "Let's talk about whatever you want," will often get little response. But the parent, who is around the child a good deal of the time and is attentive to what the youngster is saying and doing, will find there can be very meaningful communication between them. Just being with a child for a sufficiently long period of time may offer him the opportunity to discuss whatever is on his mind without feeling as if it is being dragged out of him by a harried parent wanting to get the whole thing over with as soon as possible.

I recall a personal experience in this vein. A number of years ago, I had to pick up a car I had purchased in another city. I took along my ten-year-old son and together we flew up to get the car and drive it back. On the return trip—about five hours—he asked me many questions about a variety of subjects to which he apparently had been giving a lot of thought. I felt afterward that this had been a very beneficial experience for both of us and it had come about almost accidentally. I wondered if I would have ever heard all that he had to say if we had not had that uninterrupted period of time together and how much we both would have missed in that event. It was an example of how quantity of time can be important.

About two years ago an article appeared in the *New York Times,* concerning fathers who worked in New York during the week while their families lived in Washington. One family actually felt they tended to see more of the husband and father with this arrangement than when he worked for the government in Washington. Apparently, this particular man had been working from 7 a.m. to 7 p.m., while maintaining an active social life in the evenings. It is sad from the standpoint of children to be able to say that they would see their father more when he worked in another city and was only home on weekends.

The other families mentioned gave various reasons for the arrangement. Housing and schools were better and less expensive in Washington. The children could have the advantages of suburban living. But the thing that impressed me most about these fathers was that so little attention was given to the importance of time with their children as opposed to time spent with career and social life. I think it would take an incredibly large amount of physical, material, and situational benefits to warrant having the father away from the family so much of the time.

What we really need for the sake of our children is an adequate quantity of quality time together. Whatever our situations, we should do our best to fill this requirement. The mother who remains home during the day should spend sufficient time in contact with her children. If housework must be neglected to some extent in order for her to do this, I think it would be advisable to put the work off until later. It would not be unreasonable for her to expect some help from her husband. Hopefully, in families where mothers are employed, the plans for running the household will include time for both parents to be with the children.

Fathers too should be aware of the importance of really being with their children. Colman McCarthy, an excellent journalist, wrote an amusing column in the *Washington Post* entitled "The Boys of Winter." He described his experience, taking his three young children to Florida during the Christmas vacation while his wife enjoyed a week of leisure and independence at home in Washington. At the end of the trying week, he was apparently more than ready to go back to the safety and relative tranquility of a busy newspaper office. However, he concluded his column with the following:

> But there was a new sensation in being with the boys of winter, and not many feelings of accomplishment have ever been fuller. It is strange how hotly so many men say they are seeking "fulfillment" in their work, usually

never getting it there, but worse, never understanding that they might find it deeply and lastingly in sharing their lives a little more with their children.

Teaching ourselves and others to value time is not an easy task, but time is a most valuable commodity. We should try to impart to our children the desire to use each day and to value each stage of their lives. If we can educate our youngsters to the fact that time is to be productively used, enjoyed—and always to be treasured—we will indeed be giving them something of value.

Chapter IX

Self-Esteem and Mutual Respect

There are many ingredients necessary for a happy and successful functioning life, and they vary from person to person. But if someone were to ask me the one most valuable asset a person can possess, my answer would be "a sufficient degree of self-esteem." In each of our lives, there will be difficulties and disappointments, but the child who grows up with a good feeling about himself will become the adult who can enjoy good fortune and cope with adversity.

Many times, while sitting in my consultation room, I have wished I could pick up a hypodermic syringe and give the child or adult a much-needed shot of self-respect. Unfortunately, there is no easy way of instilling self-worth in a person who reaches adulthood without it. And there is no by-the-numbers set of instructions we can give parents to insure that their offspring will grow up with an adequate degree of self-esteem. Nonetheless, we can try to isolate some of the ingredients.

To begin at the very beginning, one of the basic elements in the genesis of self-respect is being wanted. The child whose parents have given real thought to having him starts out with a great deal in his favor. This is particularly true if these parents have committed themselves to devoting sufficient time to him, and if they recognize that his care in the early years is most important. However, I do not want to imply that only infants who are "planned" will be wanted. Often, unplanned infants are very much looked forward to by the time they are born.

When a baby is born, we have no guarantee as to his assets and liabilities. But an important element in his development of self-respect is for him to be accepted for what he is. I realize that this is not always simple to do. The athletically inclined parent who looks forward to having a well-coordinated child may have great difficulty accepting one who exhibits moderate to marked awkwardness.

When I talk to parents who in some ways are disappointed with their young child, I like to cite what I consider "The myth of the ugly duckling." In the Hans Christian Andersen story, a baby duckling is born, quite unlike the other young of the species. No one thinks very much of the ugly duckling, who, in turn, is unhappy about his appearance and "worth." Eventually, as we all know, the ugly duckling develops into a beautiful swan, the most splendid and beautiful animal in the pond. Parents and other adults allude to this fairy tale in reference to an unattractive child, indicating the youngster will grow up to be a beautiful woman or handsome man. Often, this does happen in the physical sense, but the person involved still does not feel beautiful, having grown up with a sense of ugliness that is difficult to shed in later life.

This is why I feel that in many cases the ugly duckling idea is a myth. After recounting the story, I tell parents how important it is that the child have the idea early in life that he is accepted for what he is, not just for what he may or may not later become. Parents seem to forget that the ugly duckling in the story was not actually part of the duck family in which he was reared, but had somehow gotten there by accident. Perhaps, the parents feel that a particular child who does not present a total picture of what the parents desire does not really belong in their family. Soon enough, the youngster picks up the message.

A year or two ago, my wife and I attended a dinner party at which we met a woman who was physically unattractive. Yet she carried herself and acted in such a manner as to let everyone know that she was satisfied with herself and considered herself beautiful. We speculated that she must have had parents who let her know from the beginning of her life that they loved her for what she was. And to them, there is no doubt that she was beautiful. As a result, she more than made up for her plain appearance with her contented self-image.

On the other hand, I have seen young women patients who are physically striking but who honestly do not think of themselves as such and are amazed to find that other people consider them attractive. Most of these women (and it applies equally to men) were not given the right kind of messages by their parents. For a number of years, I have known a young man who is bright, handsome, and an extremely talented musician. Yet he sees himself as ugly, worthless, and unable to utilize his talent. This is definitely a reflection of the impression his parents gave him during childhood. It has been tremendously difficult trying to undo this long-standing, unfounded feeling of worthlessness.

Too often, I see children with handicaps whose parents feel as if it has happened to them rather than the child. This is true of congenital conditions as well as those caused by accident or disease. Even with something as common as a child needing glasses, some parents will act as if this is a catastrophe, for it means the child is imperfect. And quite often, the parent consciously or unconsciously communicates this feeling to the child. Any youngster will have a certain amount of difficulty with a situation that makes him appear different from other children. But his picture of himself will be many times worse if he has parents who make him feel as if it were happening to them. Children who have to contend with some physical imperfection often feel guilty because of the pain they imagine they are inflicting on their parents. Obviously, the parents' attitude in meeting this is going to be of paramount importance in the child's view of the entire situation.

For any of us to have a proper degree of self-esteem, we need to feel that there are positive things about us. Yet, in seeing large numbers of parents and children over the years, in observing the behavior of friends and acquaintances, and in examining my own attitudes, I have become aware of how comparatively little attention we pay to positive attributes in each other. We are quick to point out to children, spouses, and friends what they are doing wrong. Most often, we take for granted what they are doing right. What is done correctly causes us no discomfort, and we do not give credit where it is due. We all know examples of the student who brings home a report card of four A's and one B. Instead of saying, "You should be very proud of that report," the parents say, "Why did you get the B?"

As parents, we need to be around to teach our children and impart to them what we consider a proper set of values. I want to reiterate that our very presence in sufficient quantities of time is of great importance in knowing our youngsters. Only in this way can we be there to lend support as they learn about themselves, their environment, and their concepts of reality. There will be many times when we will have to correct them, but we need not, and should not, do this in a way which will make them feel stupid, inept, or worthless. There is a great deal a person has to learn in growing from infancy to adulthood. We would all do better if we could train ourselves to compliment our youngsters and others for what they do right rather than harp too much on what they do wrong. The child who is constantly told how stupid he is soon begins to believe it.

Frequently, we react on the basis of what our children are doing to us rather than what they are doing to themselves. The child who behaves in public in a way his parents disapprove of may be told, ''You embarrassed the whole family.'' Instead, it would be better to tell him, ''You must not be very happy with yourself after doing that,'' and to show him that his behavior was not in his own best interest. If a child wins a school contest, produces a piece of art, achieves the honor roll, or earns a scout merit badge, his parents are understandably proud of him. However, the emphasis is often on their pride, as if the main reason for doing something is for the parents' reflected glory.

Certainly children want their parents' interest and approval. But from the standpoint of the child developing his own feeling of self-worth, I would prefer to see him learn that his accomplishments benefit himself. Rather than hearing from his parents, ''You made us proud,'' which, of course, will be true, I would like him to hear, ''You should be proud of yourself for what you have done.''

Many parents demand respect from their children as if it were a God-given right. After all, one of the Ten Commandments instructs, ''Honor thy father and thy mother.'' A friend recently mentioned to me that this commandment is really directed toward parents. His reasoning is that if a parent conducts himself properly toward his children and respects them as developing human beings, the offspring will respect themselves and, hence, their parents. The model we present to our children will be one of their most important learning experiences. We need to think about what that model is and what it should be. Respect will be earned and undoubtedly received by parents who respect their children.

We should continually keep in mind the uniqueness of each child and make every effort to convey to him that he is a person of great value no matter the extent of his capabilities or limitations. This is particularly true where there is more than one child in a family, for there is a natural inclination to make comparisons between children. It is bad enough when children encounter these comparisons from teachers who have had the child's older brothers or sisters. That older sibling's performance often becomes the standard by which the younger one is judged. As parents, we would do well to look for and encourage the difference in our children rather than expect that, because they are in the same family, they should all be cut from the same proverbial piece of cloth.

If parents wish their children to respect themselves and respect their elders, it is important for the children to see that their parents respect one another. It is certainly not useful for a child to hear his father tell his mother, "He must get that bad habit from your side of the family." A youngster who constantly hears this kind of thing from his parents is likely to lose respect for them. And in the end, he will not think much of himself, since he realizes that he is a product of both.

There are certainly times when the normal drive toward healthy emotional development in a youngster is interfered with because of the problems and behavior of his parents. In practicing child psychiatry, I have often noticed that a child who is brought in for evaluation is really being used as a ticket of admission for his parents. They may be reluctant to seek help on their own, but they can justify getting help on the basis that the child is having emotional problems. In these situations, the youngster's symptoms may be compared to the visible tip of the iceberg, with many more family problems hidden beneath the surface.

At this point, I would like to return to the question of mutual respect between parents and children. Too many parents believe that a double standard should exist with regard to the behavior they expect from their children and their own. Here is an example of what I mean. A mother was telling me that she felt there was too much permissiveness with children these days and that she expected her children to respect her. She said, "My child called me a brat and I won't stand for it. He has no right to talk to me that way." While I think there were a lot worse ways this youngster could have shown his anger, I could still agree that the child should not have talked to his mother in such a fashion. However, this mother's next statement made me change my mind. She declared, "Now it is all right for me to call him a brat because I'm his mother. But I won't allow him to say it to me." It was difficult to convince her that such a double standard was wrong. In effect, she was expecting her child to control his behavior in a way that was superior to her own self-control.

For a mother to set one standard of behavior for herself and a completely different standard for her child is unreasonable and negates the whole concept of children learning by personal example. We all act from time to time in ways that may be considered juvenile. But to excuse it in ourselves while at the same time condemning it in our children is downright preposterous.

A seventeen-year-old boy became involved in a shouting confrontation with his parents over an issue on which they disagreed. When the battle had subsided, the boy came to them and said, "You know, it is unreasonable for you to expect me to act more mature for my age than you are acting for yours." His observation was an accurate one. We, as parents, will earn more respect from our children by our behavior than by our unsupported words. One cannot expect to receive genuine respect by edict—fear perhaps, but not respect.

There is another aspect to relationships between parents and children which frequently comes up in my discussions with them. That is the matter of appreciation. The mother of one of my young patients was telling me that she came from a small town in an eastern industrial state. A large number of the young people leave that town each year looking for better job opportunities in the bigger cities. When they do, they usually send large gifts back to their parents—items like television sets and major appliances. In some ways, this appears to be a noble act on the part of these young people. What bothered the woman who told the story was that the parents believed their children owed them a considerable amount for what they had done for them. She remarked that she remembered looking at her own son when he was an infant and saying, "You don't owe me a thing for having given birth to you and taking care of you."

In the opening chapter of this book, I wrote that no child can decide whether or not to be born. The mere fact that parents have a child and take care of him should not, in and of itself, make them feel that the child owes them something. The obligation to take care of the child is theirs and should be fulfilled by them in accordance with their abilities and means. I believe that in most cases, if a child is taken care of willingly and lovingly, he will respect his parents and himself, and will want to look out for his parents rather than being expected to do so.

However, what I constantly hear in my office, in my neighborhood, and at social gatherings is the complaint that, "Our kids don't appreciate anything we do for them." I know that I personally have been guilty of harboring these sentiments on occasion, but I have tried to make the effort to "straighten myself out" on that score. Why do I say that parents should not expect their offspring to appreciate what they do for them? I believe that parents have the right and the obligation to decide what they do for their children and what they give to their children. It is up to them to decide what their life styles will be. No one forces them to send their offspring to private school. There is no way a child can coerce an unwilling parent to take him on a trip to Disneyland or on a vacation to the ocean. It is the parent who really makes the decision whether or not his child will go to summer camp. While legally we may be obligated to provide food, clothing, and shelter to our children, in actual practice we, according to our means, will decide what type and quality it will be.

Some parents do things for their children because they vicariously enjoy certain luxuries and benefits they were denied in their own childhood. Others do things because they genuinely enjoy seeing the pleasure it brings their children. Still others do things because the child comes to them with the complaint that "every other kid in the neighborhood" has this or has done that. But whatever the reason, the parents have the power to do or not to do, and the children will live by that decision.

With this in mind, I feel that parents should make up their minds that they are doing things for their children because they, the parents, want to. I would ask only that parents give thought to why they are doing certain things for their children. If they are comfortable with their reasons, they should go ahead, without expecting that the children must appreciate it. If the appreciation is a parent's only motivation, the action was probably unnecessary or poorly thought through in the first place. The things that we can truly hope our children will one day appreciate are the ways in which we live our lives in relation to them and the examples we set. And it is plain to see that for this to be successful, our motivation must come from a much higher level than the mere desire for appreciation.

Of course, we do not have control over everything that goes into the development of self-esteem in our children. Much depends on their natural endowments and their ongoing experiences in the world from the time of their birth. But we, as parents, are their most important teachers. It is important for us to respect their uniqueness and to make clear to them that they are far more valuable to us than any possession. We should try to view them not as extensions of ourselves, but as individual human beings who should grow up with feelings of personal worthiness. And then we will not have to be reminded how appreciative they are, because all our efforts will be reflected in whatever success and happiness they enjoy.

Chapter X

Discipline: Love and Limits

One of the problems in writing about child care is that raising a child is a unique endeavor. Yet parents seek exact directions for bringing up their offspring. Even when one knows a great deal about an individual child and his family, it is sometimes difficult to give advice as to what type of discipline should be suggested for that child. Besides the individual make-up of the youngster, the backgrounds and personalities of his parents are factors in how a family interacts. So it is foolhardy to attempt to set down a universal formula for discipline. It may be useful to record some of my observations on the subject of discipline, but in the final analysis, it is the parents alone who must use their intuition to teach their children the only really useful type of control—self-discipline.

To begin with, all children need love. It is not really possible to give a child too much love; but along with love, a child needs limits. These help him learn to control his behavior and to cope with his impulses. When psychoanalysts first began making known their findings and theories concerning symptoms produced in some people by the repression of certain feelings and impulses, there were many parents who misinterpreted the information. They decided to raise their children by not "inhibiting" them. The idea was that if the child's impulses were not restricted, he would grow up with much less anxiety. Unfortunately, some of the worst brats in the world were the result of this type of overly permissive parenting. I recall a story about a grandmother answering her doorbell and finding her four-year-old grandson standing in the doorway. Remembering his previous visits, she made a dash for the one remaining unbroken vase in her living room. But she was unequal to the race and the vase was shattered. This grandmother did not believe that it was right for her grandson to destroy her property, but his parents were firm in their conviction that he was not to be inhibited in his actions.

In dealing with the discipline of children, we are faced with a dilemma. On the one hand, we should give them the opportunity to investigate their environment, to exercise their will, and to satisfy their curiosity. On the other hand, we must begin setting limits so that, in the course of time, they develop adequate internal controls. Our problem, then, is to try to strike some reasonable balance so that the child can use his aggressive and sexual drives constructively while controlling his destructive impulses. Again, parents should remember that the intensity of these urges and drives will vary from individual to individual.

Another important thing for parents to bear in mind is that discipline cannot be separated from the total relationship between parent and child. One can find numerous examples of parents who firmly believe that children must be disciplined and who are ready to deal out the appropriate punishment to their youngsters. But in order for the punishment to be accepted by the child and to be useful to him, it must be balanced by evidence of genuine affection from his parents. Too often, I have seen parents, particularly fathers, who are quick to mete out punishment, but who otherwise devote practically no time to their child. Any child will be angry when he is punished, but he can accept it as necessary if he has a solid feeling that his parent is interested in him and really loves him.

The development of self-discipline is inextricably tied to what has occurred in the ongoing process of the child's development. For example, parents frequently complain of their adolescent's behavior. What they seem to forget is that a child does not suddenly develop a set of values and controls, but rather, what one sees in the young adult is the culmination of what has been going on since birth.

The basic trust in his caretakers from infancy onward is the best asset a child can have to help him evolve a proper set of internal controls. The youngster who has faith in his parents will be able to accept necessary prohibitions and ultimately incorporate them into his own being. This is not to say that children will always accept rules or punishment gracefully or happily. At certain ages, youngsters have a need to rebel. And if we are to be good parents, we should be prepared on occasion to be hated by our children. But the fact that a child dislikes disciplinary measures does not mean that he may not inwardly be aware of their wisdom and necessity.

Many times, adults have told me how they continually got into troublesome and sometimes dangerous situations in their childhood, always hoping their parents would step in and stop them. The problem of knowing when to put their foot down and say, "Absolutely no!" is a difficult one for parents. In practice, I see a continuum of parental behavior. At one end is the overprotective or repressive parent who does not permit the child any autonomy and thereby always treats a child like an infant. At the other end is the overly permissive or completely uninvolved parent who leaves his child bereft of necessary support. Obviously, neither extreme is good. It is one of the tasks of parenthood to find the proper middle course for each child.

In the realm of discipline, as in so much of what goes on in parent-child relationships, our example means much more than our words. When it comes to self-control, children quickly become aware of the discrepancies between what we tell them to do and what we do ourselves. One mother complained to me of how much it bothered her that her children fought with one another. She told them constantly that she did not like fighting and she felt it was wrong for them to be doing it. However, she and her husband would frequently have loud, intense arguments within earshot of their children. In view of their behavior, telling the children not to fight with each other constituted a confusing double standard within the family. Consciously or unconsciously, parents frequently expect more from their offspring than they do from themselves.

In teaching a child to control his impulses, the early years of life are extremely important, particularly the second and third years. This is the time, as we have noted earlier, that the child goes through a stage of negativism. He begins to say "no" to everything. He has a need to exercise his independent will just as he has a need to exercise his muscles when he first begins to walk. If the toddler is asked, "Do you want an ice cream cone?" he quickly answers, "No," but simultaneously makes a grab for the cone his parent is holding. It is during this stage of development that patterns of power struggles between parent and child may develop. And once established, they are likely to persist for long periods of time. We need to remember that it is normal for a youngster to be negative at this age, and we should provide opportunities for him to say no without an ensuing battle of wills.

The following is an example of how this can be done: A two-year-old may be asked by his mother, "Do you want to take your bath now?" He probably will answer, "No,"—not so much because he has a reason for not wanting to be bathed, but because he needs to exercise his will. The mother knows that she has to give him a bath, and so has created a confrontation. What is her alternative? Rather than asking her youngster if he wants to have a bath, she can say to him, "Do you want to take your rubber whale or your boat into the tub with you?" The child has a chance to make up his mind and say "no" to the boat or the whale, and the main issue of the bath is kept out of the interaction.

Another alternative might be to say, "You're going to have a bath now. Do you want to take a toy in with you?" Here, too, the child has the opportunity to reply in the negative. Each parent should try to think of ways of dealing with his child so as to minimize the potential conflicts between them at this age.

Let us stop here and look at the evolution of the child's concept of "no," remembering that it is the parent who first uses the word. When an infant begins to crawl, he also begins to get into things. He comes into contact with dangerous situations and needs to be protected. In these circumstances, it is our natural inclination to holler, "No!" Unfortunately, soon there are too many "no's," and they become meaningless.

How can parents use fewer "no's"? When the infant begins to crawl, rather than expecting him to exert an unreasonable degree of self-control, it would be better to "baby proof" one's home. This can be done by removing valuable or dangerous objects from any area within his reach. In this way, parents can reserve the "no" for important things, so that it does not lose its meaning for the child. When a child is told "no," he should be physically stopped from whatever it is he is doing, so that he gets the message and learns to control certain actions. Learning which situations require this type of reaction is something the parents will attain through experience and intuition.

The matter of property rights is another important area in building a young child's eventual self-discipline. Most parents are concerned with teaching their children to share. They often become upset if their youngsters are reluctant to share toys and games with siblings and friends. It is certainly true that older children will get along better and enjoy friendships more fully if they have developed the ability to share and respect the property rights of others. But this will probably not be accomplished by forcing them to share their possessions at too early an age.

For youngsters to be comfortable about sharing, it is best to allow them to feel secure in the knowledge that what they own is really theirs. Along with this, they should know that what belongs to someone else actually does belong to someone else. This is to say, parents can help lay the foundation for a healthy respect of one's own rights and the legitimate rights of others.

What can we do to help our children learn these important concepts? Probably the best way to teach children about property rights is to help them develop early on a solid feeling of ownership. If a three-year-old has a toy that his mother is constantly telling him he must share with his friends, he might question whether or not it really belongs to him. But if he learns that the toy will always be there when he wants it, he will develop the feeling of ownership and later will be more willing to share.

As part of this learning process, the child must also understand that if he is playing with a playmate's toy and the playmate demands it back, the request should be honored. In this way, the youngster learns that "what is mine is mine" and "what is yours is yours." The child who gradually sees this for himself will probably have a better ability to share than the child who has been forced prematurely to share and is, therefore, overly concerned with whether or not he will get back what belongs to him.

The ways we find to discipline our children will often depend on how we were handled in childhood, what we learned about discipline from our own parents. Some of us knowingly or unknowingly treat our offspring the way our parents treated us. Others, reacting negatively to the way they were disciplined, try a totally opposite approach with their children.

One of the age-old controversies in child-raising is whether we spoil the child if we spare the rod. During my years of practice, I have seen children who were spanked grow up to be decent human beings. But I have seen at least as many who were never spanked who grew up equally as well. My own feeling is that, while children need limits, they do not need physical punishment in order to develop a satisfactory conscience and inner control of their impulses. In fact, physical punishment has some decided disadvantages.

One disadvantage has to do with fear. Young children from about one and a half to four years of age are normally afraid of a part of their body being harmed. This is the age at which a boy may notice that his little sister has no penis, and he may wonder what happened to that part of her body. If something is missing from her, it could happen to him too. Little girls have asked, "When will I have a penis again?" showing their concern that something may have happened to a part of their body. It is at this age that children develop all sorts of fears—fears of thunder, animals, vacuum cleaners, having their hair washed, and so on—all of which may really be connected to the fear that something will happen to a part of them. To me, it seems inadvisable for parents to inflict physical pain as a form of punishment on children who already are afraid of being hurt.

In addition to this consideration, there is the question of the double standard. Parents do not, and should not, welcome being struck or kicked by their children. Yet parents feel it is their right and duty to physically strike their children in the name of discipline. We should try to put ourselves in the place of a child who is confronted by a large and more powerful figure who physically punishes him, at the same time perhaps saying, "This hurts me more than it does you," or "This is for your own good." But that same parent tells him not to strike his playmates or peers, who, at least, are his physical equals.

When I suggest to parents that there is a double standard in spanking their children, they often reply, "But isn't it true that parents have certain rights that children don't have and that parents can do certain things that children can't?" There is no question that adults have prerogatives that children do not. The bedtime of a parent need not be equated with that of a child. The parent presumably has developed a measure of wisdom and judgment that the child does not possess. In many situations, it is clear that the parent must apply rules and limits. However, when it comes to the use of physical blows of any kind, the adult is inflicting violence directly on the person of the child, and the child cannot do the same to the body of his parent. This assault on the child, then, is unfair. It is better to use one of the many other adequate forms of punishment that do not involve beating. Very often, a spanking occurs at the point where the parent has lost control of the situation. The physical punishment represents a vent-ing of the parent's anger and frustration rather than an appropriate disciplinary measure for the youngster.

Therefore, I say that it is better for parents to get a little angry sooner rather than too angry too late. For example, a parent tells his child to do a chore such as taking out the trash. The child might reply, "I'll do it in a minute," and continue whatever he is doing. The parent tells him a second, third, fourth, or fifth time. The youngster indicates that he intends eventually to comply, but doesn't. The parent becomes increasingly angry and finally blows up at the child. The chances are many of us have followed such a scenario and found ourselves uncomfortable at the extent of the anger we displayed. It is usually out of proportion to the issue involved. In the aforementioned situation, a parent, after punishing the child, will feel badly that he let himself get out of control, and then, somehow, will try to make it up to the child.

It would be far better for both if the parent showed his anger before it escalated to an unreasonable pitch. When a request is made for the second time without the child's compliance, we should at that point insist that the task be done. If this verbal demand is ignored, rather than continuing to ask and becoming more enraged, the parent should take the child by the hand and lead him to the task. At this point, the youngster may say, "I'm not a baby and you don't have to make me do this. I said I was going to do it myself." To which one might reply, "If you had done it the first time I asked, I wouldn't have had to take you by the hand." Too often, we make the mistake of trying to be calm and not showing anger until we become too angry for our own comfort.

To be good parents, we should be devoted to the principle of listening to our children and trying to understand their fears, concerns, and misconceptions. But listening does not mean we need to agree with everything they say or comply with everything they demand. Every parent has been confronted with the statement, "But every kid in the neighborhood is doing it," or "Everybody is getting one." Often, the statement is an exaggeration. Even if it is true, however, it would be well for a child to learn that the important issue is what is done in his family rather than what is done in the neighborhood. I do not mean to imply that parents should not be aware of the need of their children to feel like the rest of their peers. But parents should make every effort to inculcate a good set of values in their children by word and example.

Some parents reason too much with their children. They seem to feel that no matter may be laid to rest until a child fully understands the "reasons" for a particular act, prohibition, or disciplinary measure. I have noticed parents explaining a demand to a child in extensive terms, only to have the child follow up the explanation with, "But why?" It is well for parents to give children a reason for their actions, but it is useless and frustrating to spend hours reasoning with them. The best course is to clarify the situation once and then be prepared for the possible tantrum or display of anger which can follow if the child is not satisfied with the explanation.

In some types of confrontation, the parent may become diverted from the main issue. Take the situation in which the parent tells a child to do something and the child answers back in a rude manner. The youngster may say something like, "You're so stupid," or "Who do you think you are, anyway?" The parent often becomes so involved with the child's rhetoric that the point of the parent's request is lost. An argument ensues over what the child says and he never carries out the task originally asked of him. It would be much better if the parent could accept the child's annoyance at the request and then see to it that he does what he is supposed to do. The child will benefit much more from seeing that his parent means business than from being told, "You can't talk to me that way."

Another common situation is that of the parent who asks a child, "Do you want to unload the groceries from the car for me?" Most parents phrasing such a request do not really intend to be asking if the child, of his own volition, wants to do this or that chore. Rather, they expect it to be done. I once heard a child respond to the request, "Would you like to get the book for me from upstairs?" His honest answer was, "No, I don't particularly want to, but if you want me to, I will." His mother became angry, but the child was simply answering the question put to him. If a parent wants and expects something to be done, it is much better to state simply and unequivocally, "I want you to do this." The child may grumble, but he will know that it is expected of him and that it is not a matter for debate.

Children frequently say things to us which we feel should not be said. Many parents will tell a child, "You are not to talk to me that way!" Unless some disciplinary action is taken, such statements are generally useless. Even punishment may not halt the child's exclamations. A more effective way to deal with such talk would be to respond, "You think about why you have to say that to me," thereby letting the child contend with his own feelings about his verbal barbs.

The subject of punishment is one that all of us as parents have to think about. Our views will often depend on how we were treated as children. I believe that punishment is most effective when the child knows what to expect in certain situations and is aware of the consequences of his actions. And as with any other phase of child care, fairness, firmness, and consistency are primary ingredients in a program of parentally imposed limits. I feel that it is inadvisable to suddenly punish a child for a misdeed when he has had no prior warning or indication that what he has done is considered unacceptable. For first offenses, the child should be told what he has done wrong and why the parent feels it is wrong. Again, this explanation need not be exhaustive to the point of absurdity. The child can then be advised as to what the consequences will be if the action is repeated in the future. This way, the youngster learns that he has some control over his actions and, hence, their consequences. The choice becomes his.

When it comes to discipline and punishment, it is easy to advise parents to do this or that. But when the situation actually occurs, we often find ourselves reacting with our emotions and not our intellect. Youngsters definitely need limits and, on occasion, punishment. But if we are tempted to resort to physical punishment, we should question ourselves carefully as to whether it is necessary in our particular situation, remembering that the child will see it as a confusing double standard of behavior.

Children do not expect to grow up totally free of limits, and they look to their parents to set those limits. Let us continually think about what we are doing and be reasonable in our approach. If we do, our children will accept discipline and limits constructively and will eventually come to realize that the ultimate responsibility for discipline is their own.

Chapter XI

Handling Anger

Anger is one of the more troublesome emotions we must each learn to deal with. The means we develop to cope with it will depend largely on our experiences in childhood. An important part of our job as parents, then, is to help our offspring find suitable and reasonably comfortable ways of managing their anger.

Some people are seemingly never angry. They often appear extremely timid, never saying "no" to anyone, as though they had suppressed their hostile feelings. At the opposite end of the spectrum, we find people who are always ready for a fight—be it verbal or physical. And then there are others who develop what has been termed a passive-aggressive type of personality. An example of this would be the employee who never argues with his boss about anything, but manages to mishandle the job, which in turn greatly angers the employer. This is an indirect way of handling one's anger, but it is certainly not an effective or healthy way. And as we can easily imagine, in the long run, it may be downright self-destructive.

Some people keep their anger hidden, taking it out on themselves in the form of depression or physical symptoms such as abdominal pain or headaches. A case comes to mind of a little girl who developed a severe headache each time she was angry with her father. She felt she could not display her feelings openly with him and tried to hide them. When her mother discovered this, she told the child she could vent her anger by punching a pillow. In the process of this release, the girl told her mother she felt that her headache was "melting away."

Both children and adults often manage their anger by fantasizing terrible things happening to the person they are angry with. Within limits, this is an acceptable way of ridding oneself of hostility. But there are the twin dangers of constant preoccupation with these fantasies and guilt for wishing harm to another. Children often feel very guilty about their angry feelings or frightened of what might happen to themselves or others because of these feelings.

When we consider the question of anger, we need to keep in mind the nature of man's aggressive drive. Behavioral scientists differ in their theories about this aggression. Some believe it is an innate drive in each of us, as discernible as the sexual drive. Others theorize that it is not an inborn drive but a response to frustrations that every human being experiences almost from birth. For example, when an infant is hungry, he begins to cry. Even when he is breast-fed, he cannot be satisfied immediately, and he experiences at least a short period of frustration. It is this feeling which leads to anger.

Whatever the source of aggressive energy, it is significant and should be viewed in a positive way. Human aggression, channeled in the proper direction, is the force which can enable a person to be healthfully self-assertive and to accomplish both physical and intellectual goals. But we generally tend to think of anger as something evil, or at least wrong. Children quickly get the idea that it is bad to be angry, and they may begin to feel guilt as a result. I remember seeing the child of parents who themselves showed very little outward anger. This youngster felt he was abnormal in some way because he had angry feelings and believed his parents—his primary behavioral models—did not. He was greatly relieved to find that his feelings were not unique, but were shared by others.

As I mentioned in the preceding chapter, I strongly believe that in order to be a good parent one must be prepared to be hated from time to time. Since anger results from the experience of frustration, it is natural that our children will harbor angry feelings toward us from infancy. Some of the difficult problems psychiatrists encounter arise in families in which the parents are so uncomfortable with their child's anger that they constantly give in to his every whim or wish. There simply is no effective way to avoid frustrating children, and it is important for their future well-being that they learn to tolerate frustration. Of course, it is the parent's responsibility to evaluate just how much frustration his particular child can handle at any given age. This will be mostly an intuitive process, but it almost goes without saying that the more a parent is with his child the better he will be able to gauge such matters.

If we tell a child that it is time to turn off the television and go to bed, he may feel angry because we are interfering in an activity he considers pleasurable. The fact that he is angry does not mean he should not be told to go to bed. But we as parents should try to understand that he is angry because we are frustrating his desires, just as we might be angry if something came up which interfered with a favorite activity of ours. The mature adult, we hope, has developed effective ways of handling disappointment and annoyance. The child is still in the process of learning about what he should or should not do with his feelings, and it is the job of his parents to help him.

While writing this chapter, I reached into my briefcase and pulled out several charts on young patients I had recently seen for consultation. The first was an eight-year-old boy. When this youngster was asked what he did when he was angry with his mother and father he said, "I go to my room and listen to my radio." When he was questioned as to what he really felt like doing even though he knew he wasn't supposed to, he replied, "I feel like hitting them over the head."

Under similar questioning, Billy, a nine-year-old answered, "I throw my cap but I don't write all over the wall. I go up to my room and that's it." When he was asked what he felt like doing, he commented, "I feel like taking the TV and throwing it down the stairs and I want to sock and hit them."

Susan, also nine, was brought in for consultation because she was tense and depressed. She told me that when she was angry with her mother and father she would "scream and kick and punch." As to what she secretly felt like doing, she responded bluntly, "I feel like killing them."

Six-year-old Audrey related, "I lose my temper and throw a tantrum and I try to start a fight." She felt like "killing my father and hurting my mother."

Another eight-year-old boy said, "When I get mad, I start to yell, and they yell back, and I get so much madder I feel like beating them up but I don't. I try to talk them out of what they're doing." His answer to what he really felt like doing, "Say nasty things to them and do nasty things to them."

These records were selected at random, but the comments

made by these children are representative of the anger all children harbor at one time or another. And we should realize that just as children have these angry thoughts and feelings toward their parents, so do we as parents have similar feelings toward our children. I have often said to myself over the years that no one could buy my children for a million dollars, but there have been days when I would have given them away. We have mixed feelings toward our offspring just as they have mixed feelings toward us.

Problems with anger in childhood often stem from the association of guilt with hostility. This can be as true for the child who is openly aggressive and destructive as it is for the child who is timid and displays no direct expression of his anger. Both children might feel that it is wrong to have angry feelings and, because they have them, they are "bad."

Sometimes circumstances convince children of the power and danger of their angry wishes. Under this misconception, they become very concerned. Five-year-old Johnny was punished one afternoon by his mother. He was understandably angry with her and wished she would be hurt. When, a week later, his mother did become ill, Johnny was convinced that it was due to his wishes and therefore it was his fault. It is a common occurrence for children to feel and believe that parental illness, injury, death, or separation are directly connected with their own hostile thoughts. When such an unfortunate event occurs, a parent should take special care to assure the child that he actually had nothing to do with it.

Youngsters who have a great deal of difficulty in openly expressing hostility toward their parents, may also have trouble expressing affection for them. If such a child becomes more comfortable with his anger and begins to express these feelings more openly, he also begins to be more demonstrative in his feelings of affection. It is as if the child who is uncomfortable with his feelings of anger also has to suppress most of his other feelings, including love.

Besides their feelings toward parents, children also have to deal with their feelings toward siblings. If parents came to me with stories of their children constantly showing anger and hostility toward one another, I would be concerned. But if they reported that the children never displayed hostility toward one another, I would also be concerned. Whenever I think about the rivalry of siblings, I am reminded of nature films in which young animals engage in rough play with each other. The bickering and teasing and fighting that goes on between brothers and sisters seem to serve a purpose in teaching children how to deal with their angry feelings.

Another indication of the importance of children showing aggressiveness toward one another comes from the case histories of the parents of my young patients. Those parents who report that they fought a great deal with their brothers and sisters during childhood also say that they have close relationships with them in their adult lives. Conversely, those who state that they fought and argued little with their siblings, usually say that they now have little to do with their brothers and sisters.

It is within the family that youngsters should have the opportunity to experiment with their feelings and find suitable ways of dealing with them without excessive guilt. In the home laboratory, the child learns about love and anger and how to handle each with those closest to him.

As with many other aspects of life, the child will learn most about handling his feelings by the examples we set. What we tell him about anger will certainly be important, but what he sees us do will often make a greater impression. It is absurd to tell a child, "I am not angry," when he can tell you are by the tone of your voice, the look on your face, and your behavior. We should try to be more aware of how we express our own anger and whether or not we ourselves have found comfortable ways of handling it. In some ways, it is comforting to a child to learn that a parent can be angry and yet not lose control. It is one more way a child can identify his own emotions and drives with those of his parents. He can learn that it is possible to be angry with those you love without destroying good relationships.

I remember a college student who felt that if he became angry with any of his friends, it would mean the end of the relationship. During the course of therapy, he was genuinely amazed when he found himself able to be angry with a roommate or other peer without fearing the termination of the friendship.

What can we do to help children learn to handle their feelings without experiencing excessive guilt? The basic principle is that we should give children "permission" to have angry feelings. We need to remember how many instances there are in which children reasonably feel anger. Many times, we "rational adults" wonder why a child becomes so upset over a minor thing, such as having to go to bed on time. Though we know it is for his own good, he does not necessarily see it that way. In such a situation, we may not be successful in getting the child to see things "our way," but we should let him know that at times everyone experiences anger and it is perfectly normal for him to experience it too.

The child who says, "I hate you," to his parents (and who at some time has not wanted to?) should be told that it is all right to feel that way because everyone does on occasion. It is helpful for a youngster to hear from his parents that they remember when they felt the same way toward their own parents. If a child says to his mother or father, "I wish you were dead!" he may hear in return, "What a terrible thing for you to say to me." Yet, how many of us can honestly say that we have not momentarily had such a thought? We do not actually want someone to die—we are simply extremely perturbed at that moment. Neither does a child want his parents to die. The danger in his statement arises when the parent becomes overly concerned about it.

The angry child needs to be taught there is a difference between feelings and the actions which might result, and he must learn to be responsible for his actions. For example, if a child throws a rock at his mother, he will usually be told, "You are not supposed to throw a rock at your mother." This is true enough, but the child who hears this will probably pick up the additional message that, "You are not supposed to be angry with your mother," or "You are not supposed to feel like throwing a rock at your mother." In learning to cope with anger, it is essential that the concepts of thought and action be separated.

When a child does something that is unacceptable, he should be told. But he should also be told that what is harmful and has to be controlled is the act itself, not the feeling which motivated it. The youngster who throws the rock should be told, "It is all right to feel as if you want to throw a rock at your mother because you are angry. But if you actually throw it, it will hurt her and this is definitely not all right." The child needs to learn that feelings and fantasies cannot hurt anyone—that they are normal and permissible, and different from the action that represents them.

There are circumstances where children must undergo something painful—at the doctor's or dentist's, for example. At these times, children should be assured that it is all right to feel angry. For example, during a routine physical examination, a blood count may be taken. The child's finger must be stuck with a needle, and it hurts. The doctor or parent might say to the child, "I know this is going to hurt a little and I don't blame you if you feel as if you want to stick me back."

Some children do not express their anger openly. These children may pout or become sullen without any direct verbal expression of their anger. A parent who understands these symptoms of anger can make the child comfortable. Perhaps he can say something like, "You must be pretty angry because if I were you I would feel angry. Now you can't have what you want, but it's okay to be angry with me and nothing will happen to either of us because of the way you feel."

Other youngsters may not come right out and say, "I hate you!" when they are angry—but rather, "You must hate me," or "You don't love me." Upon hearing this, a parent frequently tries to prove that the child is wrong—which is generally a useless exercise. It would be more fruitful to let the youngster know that we recognize he feels angry, and that perhaps he is uncomfortable about telling us directly. Again, we might tell him that, in his place, we would be angry with our parents too.

Again, the same concepts apply to a child's siblings. When the new baby is brought home his three- or four-year-old brother might say, "I wish you'd throw him in the garbage can," or "We don't need a baby. Let's give him away." He is expressing a natural feeling. In discussing such feelings with parents, I have often used the analogy of a perfect stranger coming into our home and telling us that he is taking over half of our living quarters. We would certainly be angry with such an interloper. To the child who has a new brother or sister thrust into his world, the feeling must be similar. Of course, he will have mixed feelings toward the new infant, depending on how the parents have handled the matter. But it is extremely important to let the child know that it is all right to be angry about having to share his mother and father with a new person who is even more dependent on them than he is.

I find that the parents who generally have most trouble dealing with anger between siblings are those who were only children. Not having lived through normal sibling battles themselves, they are overly upset when their children fight or argue with each other. Also, they often operate under the fantasy that had they had brothers and sisters of their own, they would never have fought with them. Therefore, they find it more difficult when their own children do not get along peacefully.

I might mention here a circumstance in which a child's anger is especially complicated. I am referring to children who are adopted or who are living with stepparents. When such a child becomes very angry, he may say, "You are not my mother and you cannot tell me what to do!" Such a parent should realize that even a natural child will think to himself, or say out loud, "You can't be my mother or you wouldn't treat me that way." A parent must listen to a child's anger and not to his actual words. A stepmother who is confident that her child's anger is normal can tell the child that while she is not the mother the child was born to, she is acting as the mother and will do whatever she believes to be in the child's best interests. And just as he would have a right to be angry with his natural mother, he has the right to be angry with her. If the natural parents are unknown to a child, the adoptive parents can make it clear that as far as they are concerned, they are his parents. They wanted him enough to choose him specifically, they have cared for him, and will continue to care for him. It is most important for adoptive children and stepchildren to know that when they express hostility to their parents, nothing terrible will happen to either of them.

Before leaving the subject of children's aggression, I want to mention that one of the ways children can work out their feelings is through play. During play, they can communicate with one another, work out their anxieties about certain stress situations, master developmental tasks, and express their feelings. Periodically, we hear criticisms of the policy of allowing children to play with toy guns. Parents and other adults are concerned that such play will encourage youngsters to be violent. I do not believe that playing cops and robbers or cowboys and Indians has any adverse effect on children. As a matter of fact, such play may allow youngsters to work out conflicts and rid themselves of some of their aggressive drives and urges. Later on, these same drives will be channeled into creative or productive endeavors.

In the psychiatrist's playroom, children are often given the opportunity to play out their anger by shooting members of a doll family. The result is not that they show more anger toward their siblings and parents, but rather, they usually handle their hostility in a more reasonable way when it comes down to the reality of a situation.

If a youngster acts cruelly toward animals or other children, however, we should be concerned. This is not a healthy working out of aggression through play. Such a child may be in need of professional help. But the children who enjoy aggressive play and know that it is make-believe will probably benefit by working off some of their hostility.

We can help our youngsters a great deal by remembering that it is normal to be angry. We can accept their feelings, give them the opportunity to express them, and let them know they need not feel guilty about them. A child who can successfully handle his feelings will be healthy, happy, and reasonable in his actions.

Chapter XII

Success and Failure

I have a close friend who is a professional writer. He tells me that many people, upon being introduced to him, remark, "Oh I could write a novel if I put my mind to it." My friend, who has been practicing his craft for most of his adult life, usually politely replies, "Well, you really ought to give it a try." He knows that few, if any, ever will give it a try, and I suspect that they know it as well.

Reflecting on people who are so afraid of failure that they do not make use of their natural endowments, I thought up the following verse:

> To wish that we, too, could possess
> All great rewards of sweet success
> May be to dream to no avail
> Unless we are prepared to fail.

Some individuals fantasize that they are accomplished artists of one kind or another, but do nothing to fulfill their dreams. They are content to live with the thought that they could do something if they genuinely wanted to, rather than take a chance and perhaps prove conclusively that they cannot.

I know a young woman in her late twenties who has a great deal of musical talent. She spends much of her time listening to recordings and daydreaming about becoming a concert pianist or conductor. Yet she does nothing to develop her ability. She cannot be successful because she cannot bring herself to try. And this, in turn, is because she cannot face the prospect of failing.

Obviously, when one is not "prepared" to fail, one takes away the chances of success. If a person attempts a particular task and is unsuccessful, he has to face up to the fact of his failure. As long as he doesn't try, he need not face up to that reality. But in maintaining the fiction that he is able to do something, without actually attempting it, he is losing the opportunity to enjoy the fruits of actual success.

Somehow, many youngsters get the idea that to fail is to be disgraced. Rather than believing that "trial and error" is important in determining what one can and cannot accomplish, they avoid exposing themselves to the possibility of failure. Some children complain about the boredom of school and launch a tirade against the inadequacies of our educational system. Now I will be the first to agree that many schools leave a lot to be desired, but many of the complaints I hear are from young people who are not trying. They maintain they could do well if the schools were more interesting and the curriculum better designed. I have no doubt that most of them could do well, but the primary problem lies not in the schools, but in themselves. A gripe concerning the tedium of education is more meaningful coming from a student who has made some effort and has demonstrated a willingness to try.

No one enjoys failure—it is an understatement to say that most of us strongly prefer success. The problem is that in emphasizing success, we often do not teach our youngsters that in any endeavor there is the possibility of failure, and having tried, there is no dishonor in experiencing the latter.

The playwright Tennessee Williams wrote, "Make voyages!—Attempt them!—There's nothing else." One of the most important tasks of parenthood is to inculcate in our offspring a desire to make "voyages." One may accomplish what one sets out to do or end up having put in a good deal of effort into something that did not pay off. What we should avoid is the concept that there is some great disgrace in not succeeding, and that it is, therefore, more advisable and more respectable not even to attempt a project.

A true scientist does not begin an experiment knowing he will find proof to substantiate his theories. He may work long and hard acquiring data only to find that his postulates are wrong and, in a sense, his work fruitless. On the other hand, in the process of his work, he may come upon some finding of far greater moment than that which he had set out to prove. In any event, he has tried, and this is the important thing.

Parents often contribute to their children's unwillingness to risk failure by attempting to keep them "happy" and shielding them from discomfort. They are afraid that if a child fails, it will be too great a blow to his ego. As a result, children often are not given enough opportunity to learn through experience. Too frequently, parents do for children what the youngsters should be doing for themselves. Consequently, the children are denied what I consider to be the benefits of failure; namely, the process by which one learns what works advantageously and what does not. Moreover, the child should be able to see that failing does not mean the end of the world—something his parents should keep in mind at the time.

Our aim should be to help our offspring develop the ability to cope comfortably with the vicissitudes of life rather than simply to seek "happiness." Inevitably, there will be sorrow in life. We cannot always avoid disease, death, natural disasters, or even financial reverses. Life is full of conflicts, and there are always decisions to be made. Perhaps one of the best indicators of maturity is the ability to make choices while realizing that one never knows whether the path chosen will be the best.

I believe we can help our youngsters develop the capacity to make choices. For one thing, we can let them know they do not have to succeed in each and every endeavor to keep our approval. We can show them that we ourselves do not succeed in everything. Unfortunately, there are parents who prefer to give their offspring the impression that in their own youth they never experienced failure. I know of one mother who had her daughter believing that it was immoral to fail. The youngster believed that she was the only one out of several generations of the family who had ever failed in her schoolwork and in her general behavior. Only after her mother's death did this young woman discover some letters which proved otherwise. She found that both her parents had experienced school problems in their early years. This woman's outlook might be different today had she been told about her parents' experience with failure. Today, however, this woman denies herself success because emotionally the thought of failure seems evil.

There are several ways in which we can help our children learn to cope with failure. To repeat, the model we present to them is very meaningful. If they recognize that we make decisions and are able to live comfortably with the successful or unsuccessful outcome, they are likely to adopt a similar attitude. This does not mean we must be overjoyed at adversity, but it does mean developing the ability to tolerate misfortune without falling apart or taking it out on others. If we learn from our failures, let us share with our offspring the knowledge we have acquired. Let us acknowledge the fact that we cannot be successful all of the time. We should also recognize that there are instances where there are no really good solutions to certain problems. Then we should try to make the best choice possible given the data available to us.

But the example of our own behavior is not enough. We should try to let our children learn from their own experimentation. Schoolwork is a good area to try this. Too frequently, the parent is so involved in the youngster's schoolwork that the child may cease to feel any responsibility for it himself. Parents should certainly show interest in their children's schoolwork and an awareness of the school's expectations. They should also indicate their availability if a child needs an explanation of something particularly difficult to understand. But unless a student has a physical problem (such as hyperactivity or distractibility), it is best to let him know that schoolwork is *his* job—and success or failure in it is up to him. If a youngster fails in an endeavor of any sort, our aim should be to help him learn from his failure rather than giving him the feeling that he has disgraced the family name.

There is a tendency in many parents which I feel we need to be aware of and consciously try to avoid. This is the inclination to say, "I told you so!" I am sure we, as adults, do not relish hearing this when we err. Yet, we somehow consider it a parental prerogative to toss this phrase at our youngsters. I recall the case of a nine-year-old boy who saw an expensive toy he very much wanted. His birthday was six months in the future but he insisted this should be his present. He said if it were purchased he would leave it unopened until his birthday. His parents tried to point out the impulsiveness of his action and to reason with him that the toy might not seem such an excellent choice in six months' time. But the lad could not be diverted. The toy was purchased and put away. About two weeks before his birthday, however, he told his parents he no longer wanted the toy. The natural response from the parents would have been, "I told you so!" but certainly such a statement would have been superfluous and counterproductive. By his self-induced deprivation, this young man learned more about decision making than he could ever have learned from a parental lecture.

A youngster who goes out to play in the cold without proper clothing and comes back shivering probably will not do it again unless the action becomes part of a battle between himself and his parents. It will not help much for him to hear, "I told you so." If a parent must say something, it would be better to venture the opinion, "It must be pretty cold out there and you might be more comfortable if you wear a coat next time." Too often, we do not permit the child to learn by experience. We may even tell him, "Experience is the best teacher," but we may not give him enough opportunities to make choices and learn from the consequences of his actions.

Another mistake some parents make is to offer a child a choice, and after he makes a selection, try to get him to change his mind if he has not made the "right" choice. We should avoid such a course. It is far better to impose our decision without any alternatives, if we are not actually prepared to permit the youngster to make his own choice.

We must allow our children to experience the unhappiness that comes from making the "wrong" decision or from failing at a task. We should encourage them to try again if we feel there is a chance of success with renewed efforts in the same task. We should try to help them see that, through their own trial and error, some things may be possible for them and others may not. In any case, there is no harm in trying and no shame in failing.

There is an overemphasis in our culture on striving for "success." For some people, success is equated with the acquisition of money and material possessions rather than pride in what one is doing and enjoyment of the quality of life in terms of family, friends, and other human relationships. We, as parents, must strive to educate our children to the pitfalls of such fallacies.

There is yet another aspect to be considered in relation to success and failure. Many middle-class adolescents find themselves in a difficult situation. Their parents have attained a degree of affluence, and have "made it" in a business or profession. Many of these parents grew up during the Depression. Some were the children of immigrants and others came from rural or mining communities. Many came from poor homes where their parents struggled to give their children educational opportunities they themselves never had. Consequently, whatever the younger generation succeeded in doing was usually far beyond anything their parents had done. Simply acquiring a college—or even high school—education put them that much ahead of their parents. Success, of course, is relative, and these children were much more likely to be successful than their parents.

But the teen-agers and young adults of today are the off-spring of these successful people, and they will have to try much harder to surpass their elders. Today, a college education alone will not open the doors it formerly did. As a result of their parents' financial success, many youngsters have had "the best of everything"—everything, that is, except the struggle to achieve on their own. They do not know how they might surpass their parents' achievement even though they have had the opportunity for advanced education. The fear of not equaling their parents' accomplishment is deflating to many. It would be failure, and the thought of it scares them. Often, these young people assume a philosophy rejecting "materialism" as if all money were tainted, and opting for a simple life. They roam and travel and search and eat dried beans and make pottery. This may be fine. But what they do not realize is that they may be doing this because of a fear of failure. In a sense, they are avoiding the struggle and may end up living, as Theodore Roosevelt once put it, ". . . in the gray twilight that knows not victory nor defeat."

Parents must recognize the differences between their own youth and that of their children. Successful parents should be aware of the problems of competition for their offspring. I know of many adults who are so consumed by their own careers and honors that they are seemingly unaware of the difficulties they might be creating for their children.

The father or mother who takes the job of parenthood seriously will probably be aware of a child's need to succeed on his own. Of course, what represents success or failure will vary. Our children's ideas about the subject will be derived from what we "teach" them, which, in turn, will be modified by their experiences in school and the community. However, no matter what particular criteria of success we espouse, we should help our children to realize that in order to succeed, one must also be prepared to fail.

Chapter XIII

The Difficult Child

No matter how conscientiously we take the art of parenthood, most of us really have little idea of what to expect in the way of normal growth and development in children. We often have preconceived ideas of what raising a child will be like, but these ideas come from our observations of other people's children or from our own fantasies of how we will mold the innocent babe we bring into the world. Even those who have previously been through the child-rearing process cannot be sure what to expect from the next child.

Caring for and raising a child is a deeply complex involvement with many variables. Most of us, who have closely observed children and their parents over long periods of time, appreciate the intricacies involved in the parent-child relationship. We realize that the personality of each parent, his life style, his values, his own upbringing will have a great effect on the developing personality of a youngster. Each parent's problems, and the stability of the marriage itself, can have an effect on the child.

But these are not the only factors in the business of raising a child. Some children are relatively "easy," while there are some who would create difficulties for any parent. One set of parents may be able to raise one particular type of child with little difficulty, while they would run into many pitfalls with another type.

There can be something about a particular baby that causes troubles for his mother and father. For example, birth injuries, resulting in various degrees of brain damage, may be responsible for unusual behavior patterns. Additional problems may be created by physical handicaps or lags in physical development. As the child grows older and attends school, specific learning disabilities in, say, reading or mathematics, can affect his concept of himself and his relationship with others.

Studies have been made showing that what has been called a child's traits of temperament may also complicate the relationship between parents and children. These traits are part of normal psychological functioning rather than an abnormal or pathological condition. Dr. Stella Chess and her associates at the New York University School of Medicine recorded these traits in infants and children whom they observed over an extended period of time in what is known as the New York Longitudinal Study. They observed children reacting to new persons and new situations. They noted specific attributes in children as early as the first few weeks of life, and they also observed the influence of these characteristics on normal and deviant behavior.

In their studies, they recorded nine traits of temperament:

1. Activity level. Anyone who has spent time in a nursery for newborns has observed that from birth some infants are much more active than others.
2. Regularity or irregularity in such physical functions

as hunger-feeding patterns, elimination, and sleeping. Some infants fall quickly into regular habits of sleeping through the night. As a result, their parents have an easier time caring for them and can adhere more closely to their own sleeping schedules. Other infants will wake up and remain awake during the night, placing a greater strain on their parents.

3. Approach and withdrawal reactions. This has to do with how a child responds to new situations—such as an unfamiliar food, toy, or person. Some children accept new experiences—attending school or going to a birthday party—with relative ease, while others avoid them or become upset by the unfamiliar. Dr. Chess states that this ". . . temperamental attribute may be mislabeled 'negativism' and interpreted as [a child's] obstinacy or a wish to flout his parents."

4. Adaptability. This differs from the child's initial response to a new situation. Rather, it concerns the time it takes and the difficulty or ease with which he alters his current behavior in response to the desire of his parents or others. Many children require repeated exposure to a changed situation before they can successfully adapt to it. Others can make the desired transition almost immediately.

5. Quality of mood. We speak here of the amount of pleasant, joyful, happy behavior in contrast to unpleasant, unfriendly behavior or crying. One can easily see that if a child tends to react to most problems with whining or fussing, he is likely to provoke negative reactions in his parents or friends, which, in turn, leads to more difficulty.

6. Intensity of reaction. One child who is happy may simply smile while another will laugh out loud. One

unhappy youngster may simply pout while another will let it all out in an intense verbal outburst. And still another child may show almost no outward signs of unhappiness though he feels as unhappy as the first two.

7. Threshold of responsiveness. This involves the level of stimulation necessary to produce a discernible response to sensory stimuli and social contacts. Children vary greatly in their awareness of differences in taste, smell, sights, and sounds.

8. Distractability. This is defined as "the effectiveness of extraneous environmental stimuli in interfering with or altering the direction of the ongoing behavior." If a child is easily distracted by random things going on around him, it may be difficult for him to complete tasks. At school age particularly, such a characteristic can present problems.

9. Attention span and persistence. This relates not only to the length of time a child pursues a particular activity, but also whether or not he continues in the face of obstacles. The child with a short attention span gives up easily, while the child with a longer one will stay with it a greater length of time and, if he is persistent, he will return to it after being interrupted.

Dr. Chess is careful to note that these temperamental attributes do not exist in isolation from one another. Most children tend to fall into one of three major groups, identified by certain characteristic traits. One group may be described as "easy children." They are ". . . predominately positive in mood, highly regular, readily adaptable, low or mild in the intensity of their reactions, and usually affirmative in their

approach to new situations." These are the infants who
". . . quickly establish predictable sleeping and feeding
schedules, smile at strangers, and readily accept unfamiliar
foods." Dr. Chess notes that these youngsters usually produce favorable responses in others and therefore tend to experience the world as a pleasant and accepting place. "As a
group, they do tend to develop proportionally fewer problems
than other youngsters."

Then there are the "difficult children" who are ". . . ir-
regular in their biological functions, have predominately negative responses to new stimuli, are slow to adapt to environmental change, and have a high frequency of negative mood
expressions and intense reactions." These are infants whose
feeding and sleeping schedules are not predictable. They
". . . initially reject new foods or toys, require long periods
of adjustment to altered routines, and fuss more readily than
they accept pleasure." They respond to frustration with violent tantrums. Obviously, these children require unusually
tolerant and persistent handling on the part of their parents.

The data in Dr. Chess's study shows that such children
have the greatest possibility of developing behavior problems. In fact, approximately seventy per cent of the children
in this second temperament cluster developed some sort of
noticeable problem. While these children constituted ten per
cent of their study sample, they accounted for twenty-three
per cent of the group later identified as having behavior problems.

Within this group, the sources of stress on the child ". . .
are the demands for socialization, that is, for altering sponta-
neous responses and patterns in conformity with the standards
of the family, school, or peer group." A child in this cate-
gory is able to adapt to ". . . step-by-step demands for normal socialization" when ". . . the parents can maintain con-

sistent approaches based on an objective view of the child's reaction pattern.'' While it may take him longer to learn the rules, once he does, he can function effectively.

The study goes on to state what I think is an important consideration: that ''. . . there is no evidence that parents of difficult children are essentially different from other parents or that they are responsible for the temperamental characteristics of their offspring.'' It is true, however, that attitudes and practices which are satisfactory in handling most children are sometimes inadequate in promoting adaptation and socialization with a minimum of stress in the difficult child. ''Many parents react to the problems involved in the management of such a child with resentment, guilt, or a feeling of helplessness. A vicious circle is thus formed.''

Finally, there is a third temperamental type, ''. . . characterized by a combination of negative, though mildly intense, initial responses to new situations with gradual adaptation after repeated contact with the stimulus.'' These children are often thought of as ''slow to warm up.'' For them, it is particularly stressful to ''face insistent demands for an immediate response to a new food or a new school. Pressure for quick adaptation typically intensifies the child's tendency to withdraw, and a negative child-environment interaction may be set in motion. But if a parent or teacher recognizes and accepts slow adaptation as part of a child's reactive style and gives him patient encouragement, he will ultimately become interested and involved.''

Dr. Chess stresses that the specific features and patterns of temperament play important roles in the development of behavior disorders in children, but temperament alone does not produce a psychological disturbance. Problems do arise because of the dissonant interaction between the child, with given characteristics of temperament, and the members of his family, as well as between the child and other significant people in his life.

I have quoted rather extensively from the study of Dr. Chess because I feel it is important for us to be aware of the innate differences in newborn infants. We are continually exposed to various theories of personality development and also to a variety of "schools" of psychotherapy, but the actual observable differences in infants are not theoretical. They can give us valuable information to help our offspring along the complicated process of human growth and development.

Parents should be aware that different infants will react in vastly different ways to the various stresses and stimuli they encounter as they grow. We might say that there is no "normal" way for an infant to react. Rather, there is a wide range of possibilities, most of which indicate no specific physical or psychic disorder. New parents will be best equipped for the task ahead if they keep this concept firmly in mind.

Let us return now to the dilemma of the young mother, perhaps ill-prepared for the job of motherhood, who must cope with the problems of raising a child. In spite of her lack of experience, she can, by patience, trial and error, and stick-to-it-iveness, help her child develop into a fine adult. Obviously, her husband's attitude toward her and the extent of his interest and activity in child rearing will greatly influence what goes on within the family as well.

My years of practice in pediatrics and child psychiatry have convinced me that young adults do not turn out the way they do, however that happens to be, by "accident." And nowhere is this more the case than with what can be classified as the difficult infant and child. What follows is a case history of a young man, now twenty-three, whom I have known since he was an infant. I think this story clearly shows the tremendous significance of his parents', and especially his mother's, care throughout his childhood.

Elizabeth Clarke was twenty-four years of age when her first child was born. She was a bright, attractive woman who had worked for several years as a high school teacher. She was popular with her students and well-respected by her colleagues. Elizabeth had other talents besides teaching. She wrote well, and eventually, she would produce and direct a syndicated radio program. She put her personal aspirations aside, however, where raising her children was concerned.

When her baby was due, Elizabeth stopped teaching in order to stay at home and care for him. Her husband, Raymond, was a physician just completing his residency and much of his time was spent starting his new practice.

Jimmy Clarke was a difficult child even before birth. His mother's expected date of delivery came and went as if the infant was stubbornly resisting being born. Finally, three to four weeks after the predicted date, the obstetrician suggested inducing labor. Both labor and delivery were difficult.

When the baby was born, his face appeared battered and swollen—like a prizefighter who had remained too long in the ring. He was irritable, slept poorly, and had long periods of colicky crying. These periods persisted past three months—the usual time for this difficulty.

Jimmy's mother discovered that a pacifier was one of the few things that would quiet him. Her physician husband questioned the advisability of this, but she backed her argument with an article in a medical journal which recommended pacifiers for irritable babies. Jimmy also was quieted by being carried on his mother's shoulder. He hated to be put down. Elizabeth felt as if her left shoulder was becoming lopsided from carrying him, but sensing his need for the comfort of this tactile experience, she continued.

Jimmy also had difficulties of a physical nature. It seemed that from birth he had a cold every month—his nose was always stuffed up or runny. At nine months, he had an ear infection which kept him up for several nights in a row. Two months later, the infection recurred, and he had a severe penicillin reaction.

By eight months, Jimmy's colicky crying stopped, but he developed a volatile temper. He also had an inordinate amount of trouble going to sleep. He was somewhat slow in his physical development, which caused his parents concern, but at nine months, he began to crawl fast, examining everything around him.

At the age of eleven months, when he was physically able to do more, his mother commented, "What a hyperactive baby! Jimmy is a nervous wreck and so is his mother." Sedatives were of little use. A child psychiatrist prescribed a stimulant drug often effective in calming hyperactive children, but with little success. His irritability continued.

By the age of seventeen months, Jimmy was still having trouble sleeping. His crying had diminished, but now he screamed for attention. He did not care for toys, preferring to play with any household appliance he could get his hands on. While he said occasional words, he could not yet form complete sentences. Along with being very active, Jimmy was awkward for his age and was constantly falling down and running into things. Elizabeth began to wonder what she was doing wrong. She felt that somehow the fault must be hers since Jimmy was so much harder to handle than the children of her friends.

When Jimmy was a year and a half, his parents took one of

their few vacations, leaving him with his grandmother. Upon their return, Jimmy absolutely refused to go to bed before eleven or twelve o'clock at night, and then insisted upon sleeping on the floor. His mother consulted the pediatric psychiatrist. The doctor explained that Jimmy was a hyperactive child, that he was constitutionally born that way, and that his intense activity, his irritability, and his late speech development were all part of the picture.

The doctor made various suggestions, which Jimmy's mother followed. He felt that the sleep disturbance might have something to do with the child's being frightened of his room, so Elizabeth changed the room around and decorated the crib with colored tape and pictures. She changed Jimmy's whole routine and gave him a warm bath before bedtime. She gave him new toys in an effort to have him "play out" his problems during the day. Thyroid medication was prescribed in an effort to control his hyperactivity.

A few months later, the situation had improved somewhat. Jimmy would go to bed by eight or nine o'clock, but his parents had to read to him and stay there until he fell asleep. His eating habits were extremely erratic. He resisted attempts at toilet training. He wanted to be outside running every day, and when he had to stay inside on rainy days, he was miserable.

By twenty-two months, Jimmy had begun to talk in earnest and was putting several words together to form sentences. A little past his second birthday, he began going to sleep without too much fuss. He was still highly strung, however, and became extremely frustrated when something did not go his way. Often, he cried over seemingly minor occurrences. Outside, he was difficult to manage—he ran in every direction and could not learn the dangers of running in the street.

By two and a half, Jimmy was again becoming more unmanageable, and medication was once again prescribed. On one occasion, he painted the bathroom with nail polish and an eyebrow pencil. Toilet training was still a problem. He wanted nothing to do with it. During all this time, Dr. Clarke was very busy with his work which placed much more of the burden of dealing with Jimmy on Mrs. Clarke.

When Jimmy was three and a half, his brother was born, which seemed to make him worse. He whined and cried constantly, and his mother felt as if she had failed miserably with him. Two months later, he was started in nursery school, but this proved to be another trauma. He had to be taken to school forcibly, and would not let his mother leave him. After staying each day for a month, she finally began leaving him even though he became extremely upset. However, after he got over these initial feelings, he suddenly began enjoying the school.

At nursery school, Jimmy did not like to participate in the planned activities, preferring instead to play with a single child in some quiet pursuit such as the sandbox or riding a tricycle. He seemed to be getting over some of his physical fears and had begun to venture onto the jungle gym. He also went to the dentist without fuss and showed no fear before or after the experience.

Despite all her difficulties with him, Mrs. Clarke began to note that, once Jimmy began speaking, he developed an excellent vocabulary quickly and his mind seemed to "leap ahead all the time." At fifteen months, he loved to hear nursery rhymes, and wanted them read over and over. At age two, he began listening intently to records and loved all stories, especially those having to do with trains and trucks. And at four and a half, he still greatly enjoyed being read to. Though he could not yet read himself, he would memorize long passages from books he had heard several times and recite them to whomever would listen. His mother often commented on these literary tendencies and encouraged them.

Jimmy started kindergarten when he was four and a half. As had been the case with nursery school, he had a good deal of trouble separating himself from his mother. For the first few weeks, Elizabeth rode along with the car pool, gradually becoming more firm about having Jimmy go without her. As might be expected, he resisted at first, but soon went to school with little difficulty.

While he adapted to school, Jimmy was still quite difficult to handle at home. He had periods of depression followed by stretches of hyperactivity. Much of the time, he would sulk, whine, and demand his own way. But along with this, by his fifth birthday, his mother noted, "His mind is extremely alert, and his vocabulary tends to become so adult that he is quite amazing. With all his unhappiness, he does have times of complete peace and satisfaction. Then he is very lovable and his brilliance stands out forcibly. His emotional and mental development still seems to be years apart."

By the end of the second grade, Jimmy received a report saying he had blossomed out a great deal and was going ahead academically at full tilt. Socially, he was also beginning to relax. "He makes a production of not wanting to play baseball," his teacher wrote, "but will readily offer to umpire the game. . . . His memory for facts is staggering, and although he appears to be inattentive, he is actually all ears."

Jimmy's preference for umpiring rather than playing the game was tied up with another aspect of his development. Like many hyperactive youngsters, he was awkward and rather uncoordinated for his age. As a young child, he had used both his right and left hands, eventually ending up favoring the left for most activities. His father described him to me as "throwing equally poorly with either hand." In our culture, where sports activities play so influential a role in a young boy's life, Jim was at a definite disadvantage.

Despite Jim's lack of physical ability, Dr. Clarke was anxious to make sure that his son would not feel left out in this area. They went to numerous athletic events together, and interestingly, Jimmy compensated for a weakness with a strength—he memorized his local baseball team's entire roster before he was four and a half.

In the third grade, Jim was fortunate enough to have a teacher whose influence had a profound effect on him. As I noted earlier, Elizabeth Clarke had been aware of her son's interest in stories and of his exceptionally strong imagination and use of language. His third-grade teacher, who spent much of his spare time acting in community and regional theater, decided to convey his own love of books to the ·class through serious literature. He explained the plot and concept of a book or play to the class and then they looked at it themselves. The experiment was successful beyond even the teacher's hopes, and the class jumped eagerly into whatever he gave them. Astoundingly, by midyear, these boys and girls, who only two years earlier had learned to read, were reading *Hamlet, The Merchant of Venice, A Midsummer Night's Dream,* the *Iliad,* and a simplified version of the Old Testament.

Perhaps the most impressed in the entire class was Jim. He came home and regaled his parents with the exploits of whatever character he read that day. A local college was doing a full season of Shakespeare, and Jim accompanied his teacher to each performance. From that year on, Jim's interest in literature and writing never abated.

Elizabeth continued to be aware of her son's interest in literature and did everything she could to encourage it. When he was in seventh grade, she arranged for him to participate in a local university's educational radio program for children, and two years later, Jim decided that he would like to be a writer, taking as his model a well-known television writer-producer. His interest in writing continued through high school and college and, today, Jim is a successful free-lance writer and aspiring novelist.

Jim has come a long way, considering the physical and temperamental problems with which he and his parents—particularly his mother—had to cope. A number of years ago an article appeared in *Look* magazine which described the behavior of a three-year-old child who subsequently went on to become a severely disturbed young adult. When Jim's parents read this article, they commented to me on how much it sounded like their own son's behavior at that age. We do not know all the reasons why a child with such behavioral problems will turn out one way or another, but we can be fairly certain that when a child of this type turns out well, it is largely attributable to the time and attention given by devoted parents.

At the time that Jimmy Clarke was growing up, his parents did not have such information as that in the New York Longitudinal Study. They were not as aware then, as some of us are today, of the wide range of infant and child behavior that is not really abnormal, and they were not prepared for the type of temperament their son displayed. Elizabeth at times thought she was the cause of Jimmy's erratic behavior.

However, as we look back over the history of this young adult, we can see that his make-up from birth, over which neither he nor his parents had any control, was an important factor in most of his problems. Elizabeth, by her constant care, devotion, and presence, was the greatest and most positive factor in his overcoming so many of his handicaps. I can easily speculate that with different, or improper, parental care, a child such as Jimmy might just as easily have "gone the other way." Mrs. Clarke's awareness of Jimmy's liabilities and assets and her encouragement of his interests and capabilities enabled him to develop self-esteem and a confident identity of his own.

For any mother, raising an infant is often a tedious and trying job. For Elizabeth Clarke, it was a frustrating, difficult undertaking. But her dedication and sacrifices were worthwhile. Because of her, her son was able to overcome adversity which he might not otherwise have been able to conquer. He is truly an example of "the child as a work of art."

Chapter XIV

The Handicapped Child

While the raising of any child is a complex endeavor, the problems are greatly increased when a youngster has a handicap of some kind. All children need attention and understanding, but the child who has a physical or mental disability has a greater need. He may have to be dependent for longer and to a greater degree than his unencumbered sibling or peer.

Parents of a severely handicapped child often have troublesome guilt feelings which must be worked out if they are to be in the best position to help their offspring. Some feel they are to blame if a child is born with some impediment. The parent may believe that the congenital defect resulted from some real or imagined misconduct on his or her part.

It is not unusual for parents of a severely handicapped child to have wished at some point that the infant had died. They may then feel guilty for having had such a thought. Some parents may question their ability to adequately raise a handicapped youngster. Others may feel ashamed that they did not give birth to a normal baby. And many will feel angry that fate dealt them this unkind blow.

The fact remains that feelings and problems caused by a child's disability can create additional stress for parents and children. I think it is important that these parents recognize their feelings as normal. Rather than telling them they should not feel the way they do, we would do well to allow them to air their anxieties and frustrations. Rarely is a parent actually responsible for his child's disability. But the parent may need the opportunity to grieve over the fact that the child was born handicapped. It is better for such a parent to recognize that he or she has a temporary death wish about the child than to try to repress these thoughts. In denying such thoughts, a parent might prevent himself from helping a youngster because of feelings of rejection or guilt. There is a tremendous and often unrealized capacity in most individuals to compensate for defects and deficiencies, and competent parents can be of inestimable help in bringing this out in their offspring. The child's ultimate ability to accept his handicap and to find ways to compensate for it will be influenced in a large measure by his parents' attitude.

Many children are born with handicaps, while others acquire impairments as a result of illness and injury. In the case of injury, children generally receive adequate medical care, but in many instances, not enough attention is given to the resulting emotional problems. Were the attending physicians and staff more aware of these problems, preventive measures could be taken to help a child better cope with his situation. The time and effort required to prevent emotional problems at the time the child is injured will be considerably less than that necessary to correct those problems later on. As the following case will show, a relatively brief period of psychotherapy can be extremely helpful in the subsequent successful adjustment of an injured child.

Eddie, seven years old, was playing with his eight-and-a-half-year-old brother Alan on the street in front of their home. They were both struck by a car and Alan sustained relatively minor injuries. Eddie, however, suffered multiple fractures of his right leg, requiring hospitalization and traction. Unfortunately, despite all the doctors' efforts, gangrene developed in Eddie's leg. The orthopedic surgeons at the hospital decided it would be necessary to amputate the leg above the gangrenous area. Even without knowing the extent of his injury, Eddie had been depressed since the time of his admission to the hospital. After the decision was made to amputate, the surgeons called the psychiatry department and asked if they would inform Eddie about the surgery.

There was little time available prior to the operation, but one of the hospital's psychiatrists immediately responded and came by to visit Eddie in his ward. As he approached the boy's bedside, he encountered a silent, sullen, very depressed young boy. He attempted to strike up a conversation with Eddie, but the effort was fruitless.

He then showed Eddie a male doll he had brought along with him and said, "Eddie, do you see this doll? Well, this little boy hurt his leg, and the doctors tried to fix it, but they couldn't, and it is getting worse. If they let the leg stay the way it is, the boy will get very sick and he may not live. But if they take off the sick leg, he will get better, and the doctors know they have to take the sick leg off. Then the boy will get better and be able to go out and do the things he did before.

"Now Eddie," the psychiatrist went on, "you got hurt and your leg is sick like the doll's leg, and the doctors will have to operate and take off the sick part of the leg so you will not get sicker. And then afterward you will get well again."

At this point, the young patient began to cry and said, "I don't want them to take my leg off!" The doctor told Eddie he understood how he felt and that no one wants to lose his leg. He said that if it had happened to him, he would be just as angry. But he also told him it was absolutely necessary that the operation be performed so he could get well, and that even though Eddie didn't want it to happen, it would have to be done.

The child objected strenuously, became even more depressed than before, and expressed anger that he had to lose his leg while the doctor got to keep his own. But at least he had been told what was going to happen to him and why. It is essential to give youngsters an explanation of the medical procedures to be performed in terms they can understand. They should be told what will be done to them, why, and, if possible, what effects a particular illness, injury, or operation will have on their later functioning.

Eddie came through the operation well, but as might be expected, continued to be extremely depressed. After a few days, when he was sufficiently recovered, Eddie was taken down to the playroom in the psychiatry department. In this setting, children were given the opportunity to talk about their concerns and to play out their feelings with the toys and materials in the room.

In the course of several sessions, Eddie talked with the psychiatrist about how angry he was at losing his leg. He expressed particular resentment toward the surgeon who had performed the operation. In the playroom, Eddie set up a doll dressed as a doctor and shot him repeatedly with a water pistol and dart gun. After ridding himself of the pent-up anger, Eddie indicated that he really liked the surgeon and understood that the operation had to be done to preserve his health.

On the ward, Eddie's mood improved and he was no longer so depressed. He was cooperative with the interns, nurses, and orderlies and maintained a warm and friendly relationship with his doctor. Upon leaving the hospital, he was given a peg leg and shown how to use it.

When he returned home, Eddie was not treated any differently from the other members of his family. Although they displayed understanding for what he had been through, they did not convey pity. According to his mother, once he was home and had readjusted, he was "as active as the next child and he even played baseball on his peg leg."

About two years after the operation, his parents took Eddie to an amputee clinic where he was fitted with a prosthesis (artificial limb) to replace the peg leg he had been using. He adapted well to his prosthetic device and participated in all activities in his school and neighborhood. The only time he was bothered about his condition was when his prosthesis was being repaired and he had to rely on crutches. The children stared at him and made him uncomfortable. But generally, he was described as a happy, active boy who had many friends.

Besides the physical handicap resulting from his accident, Eddie had to contend with other factors which would be considered handicaps by many people. His family was poor and black. His parents were uneducated. But he had the great advantage of having a mother and father who were devoted to him and his siblings. They accepted Eddie the way he was and treated him as if he did not have a physical handicap. He received the same care, attention, and discipline as his uninjured siblings.

While the psychotherapy Eddie received was not of long duration, it was tremendously valuable in giving him the opportunity to vent his anger and to acquaint himself with his new situation. This helped him over his depression and enabled him to function as a "whole" child again even though he had lost a leg. Undoubtedly, the fact that his feelings were in good shape when he left the hospital helped his family to respond in the constructive and supportive manner they did.

Eddie is now in his late twenties. Despite the economically disadvantaged environment from which he came, he has been able to go to college and graduate school and is now an attorney. He has children of his own who are benefiting from the kind of parenting he received from his own mother and father. Because of the efforts of his family and doctors, Eddie's outlook and self-image has remained intact, and he has been able to live his life relatively unscathed by the trauma.

When a child is handicapped, his parents may experience a gamut of emotions and reactions. These must be faced and resolved in order that the parents can be in a better position to aid in what may be a more complicated course of growth and development than that of the "healthy" child.

There are certain pitfalls to be avoided by the parents of a handicapped youngster. For one thing, the parents may be reluctant to set limits for such a child. Yet for the sake of other children in a family, the handicapped child should be treated, whenever possible, like his peers and siblings. And proper discipline is part of such handling.

There is another area in which parents of handicapped children may create difficulties. Depending on the nature of the child's disability, they may have to devote an inordinate amount of time to his care both at home and on trips to hospitals, clinics, and the like. They may also devote more time to the handicapped child because of guilt feelings. In the process, other children in the family may feel—and often rightfully—that they are relatively neglected. Parents should try to be aware of this, and insofar as is possible, should be sure the needs of their healthy offspring are met. It is also bad for the impaired child to get much more attention than his siblings—if this attention is more than he actually needs. This will only make him feel more different from the other children and stand in the way of his efforts to be as much as possible like the others. In those circumstances where the additional time devoted to him is necessary, this should be explained to his sisters and brothers, and the parents should allow the healthy youngsters to express their own annoyance over the lack of attention.

Again, we should not expect children to be more mature than we would be if faced with a traumatic situation. If a handicapped child is angry about what happened to him, he should be permitted to express his anger, and we should let him know that we would feel exactly the same way.

It is perfectly natural for a handicapped child to ask, "How did I get this way?" If it is a congenital handicap and the child is very young, it might be best simply to tell him, "You were born this way." As he grows older, he can be given a more definitive explanation of the cause of his condition. There is one parental response which I fervently hope will NOT be given. That is, "God made you this way." Hearing this, the child may wonder why God picked him, and he may imagine that he is being punished for something of which he is not aware. The youngster who is handicapped has enough problems without the burden of thinking he is being punished for something he has done.

It will also help if the child's condition is not treated as a hush-hush topic in his home. His siblings should know about it and be permitted to ask questions. If his handicap is accepted by his family, the child is likely to accept it, and himself, far more readily.

According to the degree of functional impairment in a child, he may have a greater need for dependence than other children his age. But here it is important to make some appraisal of his capabilities in order to permit and encourage the development of as great a degree of independence as possible. The parents should determine from medical advice what the child's limitations actually are, and then encourage the child to do that which he is capable of doing. As with any child, there will be the ongoing struggle between the need to be dependent and the drive to become independent. But we must be careful that he does not use the handicap itself as a basis for a life of greater dependence than is necessary. Unquestionably, there will be problems—in some cases, great problems—and the handicapped child will need our interest, support, and encouragement to make the most of what he has. But as we saw in the case of Eddie, the child can go on to lead a full and happy life if he is shown the proper attitude by those around him.

Chapter XV

Foster Parents

Ideally, as I have said again and again, each child should be wanted, planned for, and cared for capably and lovingly by his own parents. Unfortunately, there are many children who are born into this world unwanted and who are neglected physically and emotionally; or worse, abused.

These children's lot in life is a miserable one. If they remain with their original family, they may continue to receive ill treatment. If they are removed from an abusive home environment, they are often placed in large receiving homes or other institutions. In such places, there is little in the way of individual care and attention, and deprived children need even more care than the average youngster.

Another alternative in these cases is the foster home, where the child receives the benefits of substitute parents. This course offers the best possibility of repairing some of the damage. In the United States, there are approximately 350,000 children in foster homes. These children range in age from infancy through the teens.

If the job of being a good parent is a difficult one, that of being a competent foster parent is even harder. Often the child's natural parents are still in the picture to some degree, which complicates the matter and causes confusion for the youngster. In most cases in which a child is placed in a foster home, a community social service agency is involved and a caseworker is assigned to make the arrangements for the child. In such cases, the foster parents must share with the parents, social worker, and agency the rights, responsibilities, and obligations which are ordinarily in the province of the parents.

Foster parents are in a difficult and crucial position. They have to try to supply a disadvantaged child with sufficient love and care to compensate for past deprivation and to enable him to progress physically and emotionally. Along with this, they may become attached to the child and live with the realization that he may be taken from them and returned to the natural parents or some other caretaker. The foster parent must try to give the child all the love and attention possible and, at the same time, be prepared to give the child up.

In many instances, discord arises among the foster parents, the social agency workers, and the natural parents. If foster care is to work to the best advantage of the children, a spirit of cooperation must exist among all the adults involved.

It is often difficult to find a good foster home for any youngster. It is a particularly trying problem to find one for a handicapped child. But there are foster parents who do a remarkable job of salvaging children from the ravages of misfortune and deprivation early in life.

Billy is a youngster who had the good fortune to be placed in the care of just such a foster parent—Mrs. Jones. Billy was the youngest of six children, born to a mother who had had unstable relationships with several different men. When Billy was born, it was discovered that he had what is known

as congenital arthrogryposis multiplex, a condition characterized by underdeveloped muscles and stiffness of the joints.
At the age of seven months, a physical examination showed
great handicaps. The movement of Billy's shoulders was limited. He could move his elbows forward or backward only
slightly. His hands were turned to the outside. The movement
of his hips and knees was extremely limited, and there were
deformities to his feet. The examining neurologist noted that
Billy would have to be taken care of primarily by orthopedic
surgeons and that it would be "a long and discouraging process in view of the limited muscle power available."

Billy spent his first four months at home with his mother.
His father blamed her for the handicap because she had tried
to abort her pregnancy. The mother seemed to have mixed
feelings about the child. She took care of his physical needs
but did not really become involved in the maternal role.

At five months, Billy was hospitalized and received treatment designed to relieve his crippling condition to whatever
extent possible. He remained in the hospital until he was a
little over two years old. His mother did come to visit him,
but by the time he was ready to be discharged, she was preg-
nant again, and it was decided that it was not in the boy's
best interests for him to be returned to his own home at that
time.

Plans were worked out to have him admitted to a convalescent facility. There he could receive continued physical therapy, the idea being to make him as independent as possible
so that he could eventually manage in an inadequate home
situation. He remained in the convalescent hospital until he
was three and a half years old. In this setting, he did well and
was able to walk on his own with the aid of metal braces. At-
tendants there described him as an alert, outgoing boy, but it
became increasingly evident that, from the standpoint of his

emotional development, he would benefit from a home environment.

So at the age of three and a half Billy was placed in a foster home. His record at the time stated, "Billy has developed well and is sufficiently motivated to make the most of his limited physical ability. It will probably take a period of adjustment in the foster home since he has been in hospitals for all except the first four months of his life."

When Billy was a little past four years of age, Mrs. Jones, his foster mother, consulted a hospital social worker. She was concerned over Billy's lack of toilet training and wondered if it was connected with his physical condition. The social worker talked with Mrs. Jones about the child's previous experiences. She stressed the fact that he had lived in institutions almost from birth where he had received attention from a great many adults, but had not had the opportunity to develop a one-to-one relationship with a parental figure. At the convalescent hospital, he had been toilet trained and only had accidents when he became frustrated or angry. The foster mother was told that Billy was probably using wetting and soiling as a means of getting her attention. Following this discussion, Billy's toilet training improved.

At the age of four and a half, Billy was tested by a psychologist and was found to have a normal I.Q. However, he did exhibit negativistic behavior in the testing situation. A psychiatrist who examined him reported that he seemed to have a good capacity to relate to others. He had mixed feelings toward his foster mother, but most of the feelings appeared to be positive. He was quite conscious of the fact that he used wetting when he was angry with her. He seemed confused about maternal figures and saw his foster mother as his natural one. He used the term "foster mother" to refer to his biological mother.

When Billy started school, there were additional problems. Since there was no school with facilities for handicapped children close by, Mrs. Jones had to drive Billy seven and a half miles a day to meet a school bus. She found that this meant waking the child exceptionally early and having him return late. She decided that this was not in the best interest of the youngster and, instead, began driving him the entire twenty-two miles to school each day and picking him up in the afternoon. For her, this meant a total of eighty-eight miles per day to see to it that Billy got to a proper school without becoming overly tired in the process.

Billy did exceptionally well in the orthopedic unit, and during the year, was moved into a regular first-grade class within the same school. He also seemed to adjust socially and was accepted by the other children. He received ready and willing help from his peers with the few things he could not do for himself.

When he was seven and a half, Billy was seen for psychological and psychiatric reevaluation. Testing showed him to be at the lower end of the normal range in intellectual functioning. He no longer showed the resistive behavior he had displayed during his previous psychological examination. He felt accepted and wanted by his foster mother and, in return, had warm regard for her and for his peers. Not only had he made a great deal of progress in terms of positive feelings for his foster mother, but he was also more comfortable in the direct expression of his negative feelings.

It was the impression of the psychiatrist that in the two years between examinations, Billy had made great progress in his self-esteem, his relationship with the foster mother, and his ability to function in a regular classroom.

At this time, there was some question on the part of the

social service agency as to whether the child should be moved to another foster home due to the distance and expense involved in going to school so far away. But it was felt that both the school and Mrs. Jones were important factors in the excellent progress Billy had made. It was strongly advised that Billy should remain in Mrs. Jones's home and continue to go to the same school for the coming year.

Mrs. Jones was willing to continue her driving and care of Billy if this was what was necessary for his welfare. She felt that Billy was a bright child who did not like to think of himself as handicapped. He wanted to do whatever he could for himself and would refuse help whenever he thought he could manage alone. He enjoyed helping Mrs. Jones with household chores. She expressed the hope that Billy could stay with her at least for a couple of years more, until he was better able to stand on his own two feet.

Billy has gone on to a regular second and third grade and has done well. Recently, he had to be hospitalized for another operation on his legs. He took the surgical procedure in stride and, in general, appears to be a well-adjusted boy. Clearly, he has benefited tremendously from the care, love, and devotion extended to him by Mrs. Jones. Besides being willing to put up with the long driving chores, she was also able, with the advice and assistance of her social worker, to allow Billy to find more acceptable ways of handling his own emotional impulses. As a result, he now functions normally with a strong measure of self-respect.

Billy has continued to reside with his foster mother. At the beginning of his fourth-grade year, he entered a regular school close to home, and has been making an excellent adjustment to the change.

If to be a good parent is to practice a noble art, then to be a good foster parent is to practice an even nobler one. Anyone who has worked with disadvantaged youngsters will be aware of Billy's good fortune in having come under the care of Mrs. Jones. If a more optimal situation could be found, it would be that a child have the benefit of not only a foster mother but a foster father as well.

The people who choose to become foster parents and do the kind of job that needs to be done should receive our admiration and commendation. They are doing great and crucial work. But we, as a society, need to give them more than just our thanks. We should see to it that they are given the necessary financial and emotional support which will enable them to give the foster child the care that he or she deserves.

In a meeting of the National Foster Parents Association Conference held on April 28, 1973, in Congress Hall, Philadelphia, a group of ninety-four delegates representing foster parents and concerned citizens adopted a Bill of Rights for Foster Children. Certainly, most of its contents could apply to all youngsters:

> Every Foster Child has the Inherent Right:
>
> Article I—To be cherished by a family of his own, either his family helped by readily available services and supports to reassume his care, or an adoptive family or by plan, a continuing foster family.
>
> Article II—To be nurtured by foster parents who have been selected to meet his individual needs and who are provided services and supports, including specialized education, so that they can grow in their ability to enable the child to reach his potential.
>
> Article III—To receive sensitive, continuing help in understanding and accepting the reasons for his own family's inability to take care of him, and in developing confidence in his own self-worth.

Article IV—To receive continuing loving care and respect as a unique human being—a child growing in trust in himself and in others.

Article V—To grow up in freedom and dignity in a neighborhood of people who accept him with understanding, respect, and friendship.

Article VI—To receive help in overcoming deprivation or whatever distortion in his emotional, physical, intellectual, social and spiritual growth may have resulted from his early experiences.

Article VII—To receive education, training, and career guidance to prepare him for a useful and satisfying life.

Article VIII—To receive preparation for citizenship and parenthood through interaction with foster parents and other adults who are consistent role models.

Article IX—To be represented by an attorney at law in administrative or judicial proceedings with access to fair hearings and court review of decisions, so that his best interests are safeguarded.

Article X—To receive a high quality of child welfare services, including involvement of the natural parent and his own involvement in major decisions that affect his life.

When all of these provisions are met, it will represent a major step forward in helping foster parents to do the most for "their" children.

Chapter XVI

When Parents Need Help

In the ongoing process of raising children, the average parent will need advice and help from time to time. In most instances, they will require counseling about the common, garden variety of problems. At other times, they may be faced with more complicated sets of circumstances. The people these parents must turn to are those in the so-called "helping professions."

A variety of disciplines may be included under this heading—primary-care physicians; specialists of various sorts; dentists; psychologists; social workers; educators (particularly special education); speech and hearing therapists; physical, occupational, and recreational therapists; and so on. There are many experts around; the problem is how to select the best help available.

How should a patient select a doctor, for example? In some ways, this is a difficult question because so much depends on the personality of both patient and doctor. A very dependent parent will look for one type of pediatrician, while a more independent parent will want another. The first will want, and need, a large measure of direction. The second will want a doctor who gives the pertinent information and lets the parent make up his or her own mind as to how to carry on from there.

I have found that the average layman may have unreasonable expectations when it comes to physicians. There are many people who expect the doctor to know everything and to magically be able to make things right. Reason, of course, tells us that a doctor cannot know everything. Therefore, one might look for a physician who acknowledges this fact and can act in accordance with it. That is to say, a doctor who knows when he needs additional help and knows where to find it.

The primary-care physician, pediatrician, or family doctor is a key person. He should be able to listen to what is going on and make his own observations, do what he can within the realm of his expertise, advise parents as to what other specialized help might be needed, arrange for them to get the necessary advice, and consult with the various other specialists involved in the child's care.

It is difficult for some physicians and most patients to cope with the realization that we do not have all the answers. We never like to be left with a feeling of helplessness when confronted with a condition for which we have no answer. Our reaction may be to try to come up with too definite an answer, or to drain our physical, emotional, and financial resources looking for a solution that may not exist.

On occasion, an expert will be limited by the narrow confines of his particular specialty. I can recall the case of Susie, a girl who was five years old when I saw her for consultation. She was the second of three children. Her parents became concerned when, at the age of three, she was not yet talking. Her hearing was tested and found to be normal. She was then seen by a neurologist who ventured an opinion that she was severely brain-damaged, severely retarded, and should be placed in an institution as soon as possible.

Susie, who displayed some withdrawn behavior, was taken to another city to see a doctor who specialized in treating psychotic children. Here the diagnosis was that the girl was autistic, and hospitalization and electroshock therapy was recommended. The family rejected this course of treatment and took Susie to a third city where an examining physician also concluded that she was brain-damaged. But he also believed her to be suffering from aphasia, a condition in which hearing is normal but the child is unable to comprehend what he or she hears. As a result, she would tend to ignore a good deal of sound. Susie was started in therapy with a speech pathologist and made progress, but the speech teacher felt that something stood in the way of further advancement. She suggested psychiatric evaluation, at which point I saw Susie in my office.

My impression was that there may have been some truth in each of the various views offered of this young patient. She did give evidence of behavior and actions which could indicate possible brain damage. She did demonstrate some autistic behavior, but she could also relate to another person when she wanted something done for her. She did not seem to understand spoken language adequately. Whether or not retardation was present could not be determined in light of all these other symptoms. At the time I saw her, my own feeling was that it was most important to try to get her to relate on a more consistent basis in order that the underlying problems and degree of brain damage could be better evaluated. She was referred to a mental health facility for therapy. It is my understanding that, with such therapy, Susie was able to relate better, and at that point remedial measures, such as special education, were instituted to help her compensate for her organic difficulties.

I cite Susie's case for several reasons. First, it indicates the complexities that can be involved in attempting to give parents the advice they seek. Secondly, it is the type of problem which makes me feel a great deal of sympathy for the parents who find themselves in a dilemma. Which expert should they listen to? How do they know if they are making the best decision? Where can they find a person or clinic that really has the answer?

It is my feeling that, in many cases, we never can know if we make the correct decision. We cannot start from square one and try to solve the same problem two or more different ways. We must weigh all the data and make the best determination we can. We face additional problems. When should a parent look for another opinion, and when does a continuing round of "doctor shopping" lead to nothing but frustration and depletion of physical and monetary resources? There is no easy answer.

Under circumstances such as these, I feel that a good relationship between the parents and a primary-care physician is invaluable. If there is sufficient interest on the part of the doctor and sufficient trust on the part of the parents, the doctor can be an effective partner in the decision-making process.

It is important that patients let their physicians know when they are dissatisfied. No doctor is infallible, and he should not object to consultation when it is requested and carried forth in a direct and courteous fashion. Patients should also remember that it is their prerogative to change doctors if and when they desire. For their own sakes, they should discuss with the physician the apparent causes of their discontent. Issues can often be clarified, misconceptions on both sides cleared up, and both physician and patient can benefit from the continuing relationship. This is particularly true where the interests of children are involved and difficulties arise between the parents and doctor.

A good physician may resist parental requests. Such requests are often prompted by the public media devoting attention to certain therapeutic procedures and medications. Twenty-four years ago, for example, I remember spending a great deal of time talking parents out of penicillin shots for the common cold. Somehow, they had gotten the idea that every time a child had a cold, he would not recover unless he had a penicillin shot. When reports began appearing of severe and sometimes fatal reactions, it became easier to convince mothers that not every sniffle required a shot.

Then there were instances where mothers had to be convinced to continue giving an antibiotic even though the youngster's temperature had returned to normal. A mother may be reluctant to continue medicine when the child is apparently well unless she is specifically warned of the danger of complications if the antibiotic is not given for long enough periods of time. These complications can include rheumatic fever and kidney disease.

Though the physician may be the first line of aid and information for parents, there are other trained individuals who can be of enormous help. I would like to describe briefly some of their functions, for I know from working closely with many of them how valuable their contributions can be. In many situations, teamwork is extremely important in obtaining the maximum results for the child.

One group of specialists includes those who work in the area of audiology and speech pathology. These are often referred to as "speech and hearing people." I prefer to think of them as "communication specialists," for they will try to evaluate and help with any disorder affecting a child's ability to communicate in words. This can involve speech, hearing, and understanding language.

Often the absence of speech is what focuses a parent's concern on whether there is any abnormality in the child's development. Some children will not talk at all. Others will be difficult to understand. Some may be slow in learning to speak. When a parent brings such concerns to a physician, he is likely to refer the patient to a speech and hearing center or to an individual practitioner.

Normally, the first step is that the child's hearing will be tested. Special equipment is used to determine the cause, type, and extent of any hearing loss present. As a result, a hearing aid or other remedial measure might be prescribed.

Also, the child's speech will be evaluated, and his abilities and disabilities will be noted. Remedial speech therapy can then be recommended, with the speech pathologist helping the child and the parents in dealing with the particular problem. Youngsters with congenital deformities—such as cleft palate—can benefit from the aid of speech personnel.

Some children have a specific language disorder in which they are able to hear, but unable to understand what is said. Other youngsters may be able to hear and understand, but are unable to express themselves in language. These conditions are often referred to as "receptive" aphasia or "expressive" aphasia. Children with these difficulties require careful evaluation and specialized teaching to overcome their disabilities. Much of this falls within the realm of the audiologist and speech pathologist.

A psychologist is another expert who can help parents with a problem. A great deal of confusion exists in the mind of the public as to what a psychologist does, what a psychiatrist does, and whether there is any difference between them. Part of the perplexity results from the fact that, in some instances, the psychologist may do the same type of work as the psychiatrist. The main distinction between the two is that the psychiatrist, being an M.D. or medical doctor, can prescribe medication if it is required, while the psychologist-therapist would have to refer the patient to a physician for prescribed medication.

But here we are concerned with another function of the psychologist, which is his particular area of expertise—the testing and evaluation of the individual child. The psychologist will select and administer tests of varying types and, with the results, will derive information which will help in determining the intellectual capacity of the child. He may discover unevenness suggesting that the child may do well in some areas of intellectual functioning and poorly in others. Some tests might reveal problems in perception of various types. Others might indicate the presence of minimal brain dysfunction.

In addition to the tests which measure intelligence and perceptual abilities, the psychologist can administer what are known as projective tests. These include such well-known techniques as the Rorschach (ink blot) test and others in which the child is asked to make up stories in response to pictures or other stimuli. Through this type of test, the examiner can draw conclusions about the underlying make-up of the child. The results of a competently administered battery of psychological tests are often important in the evaluation of a child's condition.

Other therapists deal with children with physical handicaps, both temporary and permanent. One group is the physical therapists. Their aim is to evaluate the child's physical problem and help him overcome the handicap to whatever extent he can. The physical therapist will often follow the prescription of an orthopedist or a physical medicine specialist. Frequently, by daily observation of the patient, the therapist can offer valuable information to the parents and doctors.

The physical therapist may test a child's motor abilities and muscle function. He may be able to help awkward children do better with their motor control. Some children need help in distinguishing between right and left. The therapist may be able to help a child with mild cerebral palsy.

There are temporary handicapping conditions which a therapist can help to make disappear in a shorter time. For example, in the case of a child who has been in traction for a month or two with a broken leg, the physical therapist will teach him how to walk with crutches until his cast is removed and will teach him the correct way to condition his upper extremities to make getting around in the cast easier. Unfortunately, there are many cases in which patients are given good orthopedic treatment but not referred to the physical therapist for important help and advice in terms of muscle reconditioning and rehabilitation.

An allied discipline is occupational therapy. In many settings, the occupational therapist or "O.T." works hand in hand with the physical therapist to enable a child to reach his highest potential, whatever his handicaps. Through testing, both the occupational therapist and physical therapist gather data to help evaluate the nature and degree of a disability. They devise techniques to help retrain motor patterns. They may design special feeding equipment for youngsters who are unable to feed themselves in a conventional way. Occupational therapists may train the parents to do things for the child at home. Often, the O.T. will have to use ingenuity to figure out ways to help the children cope with the physical problems at their own age level. They may adapt chairs, tables, and other equipment so that the parents can better care for the child at home.

Along with the physical therapists, the O.T.'s will work with amputees to help them with the training necessary for the proper use of their prosthesis. The O.T. is also involved in teaching handicapped children practical activities such as dressing, feeding, and writing. They may have to adapt equipment for schools to enable the partially disabled to do their work.

In many hospital programs, the occupational therapist provides psychological supportive programs for hospitalized children. In other hospitals, this function has been taken over by another trained person, the recreational therapist. Just as the physical and occupational therapists must earn college degrees and have field experience in their specialties, so does the recreational therapist have a four-year degree in therapeutic recreation, including field experience. In the hospital, the R.T. engages the children in activities which not only keep them occupied but also help in working out their frustrations over hospitalization and their particular illness or injury. The recreational therapist tries to get to know the particular patient and the entire group of children and tailor the activities to their needs. These therapists also function in playground and recreational centers. In many cases, the parents are encouraged to come in and participate in play with their children.

The social work profession is of great help in many situations. Although the public image is changing, there is often the mental picture of the social worker helping poor people by providing them food, money, or clothing. It is true that, in many instances, social workers do try to investigate the needs of clients and help them in securing some of the necessities of life. But the province of social workers includes much more. They play an important role in the family agencies to which people in trouble can turn for advice and direction. In mental hygiene clinics, social workers serve as part of a team that provides help for individuals with emotional problems. With adequate training, some social workers do individual and group psychotherapy. In hospitals, they give great supportive help to children and adults to enable them to overcome their fear of hospitalization. The social workers sometimes perform an important function within the school system. Here they may collect information from the student, parent, teachers, physician, and psychologist and act as a go-between in devising the best plan to meet a child's individual needs. They can be found attached to juvenile courts where information is gathered for the judge. They may operate as counselors to young people who come under the direction of the court or they may counsel their parents. There are still other disciplines which I will not go into here. The important thing is for parents to realize that there are services available to aid them in their effort to help their child to make the most of his or her natural endowment.

Chapter XVII

The Community

While the primary influences on a child's successful development are his parents, the community as a whole and the facilities it affords can also help a youngster make the most of his potential.

There is no profound insight involved in stating that a large number of children from economically, socially, and culturally deprived backgrounds get into trouble. Some become lifelong criminals. Considering the deprivation, I do not find this surprising. Rather, what I marvel at are the large numbers of persons from such backgrounds who become upstanding, productive citizens. Perhaps too many of our studies of deprived people deal with those who get into trouble and not enough attention is paid to the positive factors that enable some to overcome their environment.

Undoubtedly, a cohesive family with both a mother and a father present in the home would be the most positive factor. The physical, temperamental, and intellectual endowments of an individual child are also certainly significant in his growth and development. But there is another factor in whether or not a child "makes it" which is often overlooked. This factor is the facilities which the community has to offer—particularly its schools and recreational resources. I am not speaking merely of physical plants, although adequate plants are certainly important. I am concerned more with the ratio between teachers and students, and the relationship between them.

The subject of education is broad, and I cannot claim to be an expert in this vast domain. But in studying children over a number of years and in working closely with school officials, I have been impressed with the benefits over and above the accumulation of knowledge that certain children derive from schooling. If the child can find adults at school whom he can look up to and identify with, it may make a big difference in the way the youngster sees himself and in the goals he sets.

Fashions in education change, and various methodologies have vociferous advocates. Some say that highly structured classrooms are best, while others advocate the open classroom. Whatever the system, a great deal will depend on the personality and capability of the teacher. When we look back, most of us feel fortunate if we can recall one or two outstanding teachers who had an important effect on our thinking and development. Of course, it is unrealistic to wish that all teachers could be like this, so I find myself thinking about what else we might do to benefit children in the school situation.

An experienced teacher I know has been telling me for years that what makes for "quality education" is nothing more than a large percentage of quality students. Her point is that the children who generally do well in school come from advantaged homes. Because they come from a certain sociocultural milieu and are encouraged by their parents, these children are able to obtain a quality education. Published reports from several universities corroborate this view, showing that education alone is not the answer to poverty, inequality, and failure. To a great extent, I agree with this analysis. However, it does not erase the question of what can be done to improve schools so that youngsters derive as much as they possibly can from going to school.

I believe that the single most advantageous move would be to cut down the size of classes so that there would be one teacher for every fifteen to eighteen students. National implementation of this would certainly be expensive but, in the long run, we would accrue financial and humanistic savings. For example, we would need fewer correctional and special educational facilities. No matter how superior or inferior a teacher may be, she can probably do a better job if she has fewer students. She will be more aware of her students' abilities and disabilities when there are fewer people to share her attention.

While it has always seemed obvious to me that smaller class size should be of tremendous value, I have often heard the argument that the size of the class does not make that much difference. However, after working for several years in a psychiatric diagnostic clinic attached to the Washington, D.C., public school system, I became convinced that class size mattered very much. Our studies at the clinic indicated that cutting down class size would be a great help in reducing the number of children referred to us as problems. This is because the teacher would be in a better position to handle individual cases before they became serious or unmanageable. In this way, we felt we could cut down on a lot of expensive specialized help.

Here is an example of what might have been accomplished in a smaller classroom. Two young students were referred for evaluation. One was a boy who had been described as a "menace to his classmates, very destructive." The other was a girl, a slow learner who was very withdrawn. In this clinic, the children were seen by a psychiatrist and then tested by a psychologist. At the conclusion of these procedures, a conference was held with the teacher and/or principal in attendance. Between the time of the referral and the conference, both children had been placed in a special class of eight or ten students. The class had been set up within their school and was taught by a young and capable teacher. By the time of the conference, both children were reported much improved. It was felt that without the small special class experience, both would have needed psychiatric therapy. Some time afterward, a follow-up contact was made with the teacher. She said that the boy was still doing well and the girl had changed from being withdrawn to "acting up" somewhat in class.

I strongly believe that the job of teachers is to educate their students. I do not feel they should be psychotherapists or social workers. But I do believe that the schoolroom can provide a therapeutic environment if the teacher has the time to be aware of the individual child. And this is not the case in very large classes.

Many things could help teachers. The opportunity to consult experts regarding problems may aid a teacher in recognizing a student's difficulties in a particular situation. There will always be youngsters who present problems no matter what the class size may be. But a low teacher-student ratio could eliminate a certain percentage of disruptive and delinquent behavior simply because of the increased attention the teacher could pay to each student. The mediocre teacher would do a better job and gain a better knowledge of her students. The outstanding teacher would have the time to give a fuller measure of her talents to the youngsters who had the good fortune to come under her influence.

As a physician, I am constantly coming into contact with a group of children with special needs—needs which too often go unmet. These are the youngsters who require special education of some kind. To a large extent, we still lack the proper knowledge of how to educate children with specific learning disabilities. Even where the know-how exists, there may not be sufficient funds allocated for special education and there may not be an adequate number of trained teachers. It has frequently been noted that, as our medical care improves, there is an increase in the number of children with various cerebral dysfunctions due to brain damage. Better obstetrical procedures keep infants alive who would not have survived years ago. Youngsters may survive central nervous system infections or injuries, but they are left with the lasting effects. When they reach school age, they may experience great difficulty in some aspect of learning. In order to compensate for and overcome their deficiencies, they will need special classes and often specialized instruction. Even more than with "normal" children, one must look for and accentuate their strengths, and help them to overcome their problems. It should be the objective of the community to provide each child with the optimal opportunity to obtain education and training leading to the greatest possible self-sufficiency and self-esteem.

We should note that boys and girls today generally are not receiving the on-the-job training for parenthood that was the case as recently as a generation ago. The families today tend to be smaller and children now do not often take part in the care of their younger siblings. There are, however, experimental programs going on in some secondary schools to help young men and women learn more about child growth and development, and to help them become effective parents when the time comes. They learn concepts such as the importance of adequate nutrition for the mother prenatally and the infant after birth.

I certainly hope that now, and in the future, fathers will play a greater role in the day-to-day care of infants and children. To do this job properly, they will need more education about children. Our schools may have to be the institutions that offer courses in domestic skills, including the observation and care of infants and young children. In one local school where boys and girls are both required to take home economics and industrial arts, the cooking and related courses are conducted under the designation, "Domestic Survival." With parenthood being such an important occupation for which relatively few of us are well trained, we may need to look at our schools to enable us to "survive."

Another phase of community life which affects most of our youngsters is that of recreational activities. In numerous ways, they can be of enormous value to children. In my opinion, however, they are often neglected or mishandled.

Physical activities, such as individual and team sports, offer children the opportunity to achieve and maintain good physical conditioning. Some sports provide not only the benefits of physical conditioning, but also the chance for parents and children to be together. Tennis, swimming, and jogging are examples.

Besides the bodily benefits of sports, these activities give pleasure to children. However, too often what should be a vehicle for learning, developing skills, and having fun becomes a serious business with the emphasis on winning. Normally, this orientation does not come from the youngsters themselves but from parents and coaches.

Last fall, I was waiting for my wife outside a store in a large shopping center. On a field across the street, a football game was in progress, involving what appeared to be eleven-year-olds. I went over and joined the spectators. The children themselves were playing with enthusiasm and a fair degree of skill. But the parents and coaches were unbelievable. They were screaming at the officials and carrying on as if winning this game were the most important thing in the world. The behavior of these supposedly mature adults exemplified what is so terribly wrong with many of the Little-League-type sports programs.

In such programs, we have the means of getting children together and teaching them not only physical skills but concepts of team play, cooperation, and regard for one another. However, it seems to me that in relatively few programs is this still done. Many programs do have provisions that each child must be allowed to play a certain number of innings or a fixed proportion of the game. But in practice, the youngster who does not possess a maximum of talent gets little opportunity to improve; the emphasis on winning is too great. The adults involved become carried away with the need for vicarious victory. Instead of providing a moderating influence on their youngsters, they often give the impression that their own self-esteem will rise or fall on the outcome of a Little League game.

In our culture, sports figures have always been important heroes for children. There is nothing wrong with a will to win, but it would also be advantageous if youngsters could have examples of how one loses gracefully. From the standpoint of its effect on children, I see nothing beneficial in statements such as that of the late and much-revered football coach Vince Lombardi that, "Winning is not the most important thing. It's the only thing," or Washington Redskins' coach George Allen's "Losing is like death." Rather, we should teach our children that trying their best and enjoying what they are doing is the one really important aspect of playing the game. The pride should not come from winning, but from knowing we have done our best to try to win.

For those who want it, there is time enough when young people reach high school to put stress on the importance of winning in interscholastic sports. At earlier ages, the primary emphasis should be on recreation and development of skill, not competition. Even in private schools where the sports program is often supposed to be an integral part of the curriculum, coaches exaggerate the matter of winning on the elementary school level. I wish that parents would look into their own school's athletic program and insist that every child's needs be met in these endeavors and not just those of the natural athlete.

Parental attitudes are of utmost importance in what benefits their youngsters derive from sports. Adults have told me that as children they engaged in athletics merely to try and please their own parents. Fathers particularly should be mindful of not forcing their children (especially sons) into activities for the sake of the vicarious pleasure they may experience. The awkward child needs parental understanding, encouragement, and involvement in practice sessions to help him improve whatever ability he has. Sadly, I have often seen boys who were practically rejected by their fathers because the youngsters did not possess natural prowess in athletics. The fathers could not handle this "blow" emotionally, feeling it somehow detracted from their own ideas of manliness and self-worth.

The parent's conduct can have a beneficial or detrimental effect, even in the case of the athletically gifted child. For example, Bobby was an excellent shortstop on a Little

League team. In a closely matched and hotly contested game, he performed admirably. In the ninth inning, he fielded a ground ball and quickly threw to first base for what should have been the final out. But Bobby overthrew first base and, as a result, his team lost the game. I have observed many parents who would have been irate with the boy and by their comments made him feel worthless for being responsible for the loss of the game. Fortunately, this situation was different. Bobby's father, who frequently attended the games, put his arm around his son's shoulder and said, "You really played well today. Too bad that error came when it did." He had recognized the boy's discomfort, but was able to let him know that he had still done well and that it was no disgrace to make a mistake.

There are varying opinions about the dangers of contact sports such as tackle football for youngsters who are still growing. Several professional football players have stated publicly that they do not allow their pre-teen sons to play. Recently, I asked Dr. Charles Epps, Professor of Orthopedics at the Howard University School of Medicine, for his opinion on the question. He feels that it is acceptable for children to engage in these activities under certain conditions. Attention should be paid to the weight class in which they play. They should be provided with adequate equipment, including properly fitted mouthpieces. He also feels that a crucial factor in sports for the younger age groups is the attitude of coaches and instructors. The children should not be taught to emulate the tactics of the professional players they might see on Sunday afternoons. They should be instructed in the fundamentals and techniques that minimize the risk of injury. I cannot stress enough how important the attitude of the adults involved can be.

The community should provide recreation centers and

neighborhood facilities where youngsters can engage not only in athletics but in arts, crafts, and other activities such as clubs and Scout troops. With the proper type of leadership, boys' and girls' clubs can afford children the opportunity to deal with rules and to learn about the usual give-and-take within an organized group. In many instances, children benefit greatly from being able to identify with adults other than their parents. This is particularly true when a parent is not available or displays behavior which makes him or her a poor model for the child.

There are many ways that the community can contribute to the welfare of children. Each parent should try to become aware of the facilities and activities in his community which can aid in the evolution of the child as a work of art.

Afterword

While we are at the end of this book, I feel that really there can be no end to the subject of childrearing. With the uniqueness of each human infant and the multiple, complex factors involved in growth and development, exploration in this field could go on almost indefinitely. Also, some of our specific ideas about childrearing practices may change in the future as they have in the past.

But as long as man continues to exist there will be children to be cared for, and the relationship between parents and children will continue to be a most important factor in the development of our offspring. The art of parenthood is indeed challenging. I reiterate that to my way of thinking there is no more important job.

There was a time when couples were embarrassed not to have children. This does not seem to be true at present. We should be embarrassed, however, if we are not willing to devote the time, love, discipline, and support that is essential if we *do* decide to bring a child into the world.

I would like to end as I began, with the hope that those

who are already parents will try to be conscious of what is required to practice competently the noble art of parenthood, and that those who may be thinking of becoming parents will try seriously to consider whether or not they really want to apply themselves to a difficult but ultimately rewarding art.

Bibliography

Accident Facts. National Safety Council. 1973 Edition.

Barnett, C. R., Leiderman, H., Grobstein, R., and Klaus, M. "Neonatal Separation: The Maternal Side of Interactional Deprivation." *Pediatrics,* Vol. 45, no. 2, February 1970.

Blaine, Graham B., Jr. *Are Parents Bad for Children?* Coward, McCann & Geoghegan, Inc., New York, 1973.

Bowlby, J. *Attachment and Loss.* Vol. 1, Basic Books, New York, 1969.

Chess, S. "Temperament and Children at Risk." In *The Child in His Family,* edited by James E. Anthony and Cyrille Koupernik. Wiley-Interscience, New York, 1970

Children's Bureau. Office of Child Development. "Rights of Foster Children." *Children Today,* Vol. 2, no. 4, July-August 1973.

Emlen, A. C. "Slogans, Slots, and Slander: The Myth of Day Care Need." *American Journal of Orthopsychiatry,* Vol. 43, no. 1, January 1973.

Greenberg, M., Rosenberg, I., and Lind, J. "First Mothers Rooming in with Their Newborns: Its Impact upon the Mother." *American Journal of Orthopsychiatry,* Vol. 43, no. 5, October 1973.

Harlow, H. F. "Primary Affectional Patterns in Primates." *American Journal of Orthopsychiatry,* Vol. 30, no. 4, October 1960.

Heinicke, C. M., Friedman, D., Prescott, E., Puncel, C., and Sale, J. S. "The Organization of Day Care: Considerations Relating to the Mental Health of Child and Family." *American Journal of Orthopsychiatry,* Vol. 43, no. 1, January 1973.

Howell, M. C. "Employed Mothers and Their Families." *Pediatrics,* Vol. 52, no. 2, August 1973.

Klaus, M. et al. "Maternal Attachment: Importance of the First Postpartum Day." *New England Journal of Medicine,* Vol. 286, no. 9, March 2, 1972.

Klaus, M. and Kennell, J. H. "Mothers Separated from Their Newborn Infants." *The Pediatric Clinics of North America,* Vol. 17, no. 4, November 1970.

Klaus, M. H., Kennell, J. H., Plumb, N., and Zuehlke, S. "Human Maternal Behavior at the First Contact with Her Young." *Pediatrics,* Vol. 46, no. 2, August 1970.

Korner, A. F. "Individual Differences at Birth: Implications for Early Experience and Later Development." *American Journal of Orthopsychiatry,* Vol. 41, no. 4, July 1971.

Lourie, R. S. "The First Three Years of Life: An Overview of a New Frontier of Psychiatry." *The American Journal of Psychiatry,* Vol. 127, no. 11, May 1971.

Meers, D. R. "Psychiatric Ombudsman for Day Care." *Clinical Proceedings, Children's Hospital National Medical Center,* Vol. 30, No. 1, January 1974.

Montagu, A. *Touching: The Human Significance of the Skin.* Columbia University Press, New York, 1971; Perennial Library, New York, 1972.

Newton, N. "The Uniqueness of Human Milk: Psychologic Differences Between Breast and Bottle Feeding." *American Journal of Clinical Nutrition,* Vol. 24, August 1971.

Olshaker, B. "Pediatric Psychiatry in a School Health Services Program." *Medical Annals of the District of Columbia,* Vol. 29, no. 2, February 1960.

Prescott, J. W. "Early Somatosensory Deprivation as an Ontogenetic Process in the Abnormal Development of the Brain and Behavior." In *Medical Primatology,* edited by S. Karger. Basel, New York, 1971.

Robertson, J., and Robertson, J. "Young Children in Brief Separation: A Fresh Look." *The Psychoanalytic Study of the Child,* Vol. 26, Quadrangle Books, New York, 1971.

Spitz, R. "Hospitalism: An Inquiry into the Genesis of Psychiatric Conditions in Early Childhood." *The Psychoanalytic Study of the Child,* Vol. 1, International Universities Press, 1945.

Van Lawick-Goodall, J. "The Behavior of Chimpanzees in Their Natural Habitat." *The American Journal of Psychiatry,* Vol. 130, no. 1, January 1973.

Women's Bureau. U.S. Department of Labor. Unpublished Data.

Index